CW00642455

Who Killed Martin Hannett?

Colin Sharp is a playwright whose work has regularly featured on stage and radio. He was lead singer and songwriter for the post-punk band The Durutti Column and best friend of Martin Hannett.

Who Killed Martin Hannett?

The Story of Factory Records' Musical Magician

Colin Sharp

Aurum

First published in Great Britain
2007 by Aurum Press Limited
7 Greenland Street
London NW1 0ND

Copyright © 2007 Colin Sharp

The moral right of Colin Sharp to be identified as the author of this work has been asserted by him in accordance with the Copyright, Designs and Patents Act 1988.

Although this is a work of non-fiction, the names of some of the characters have been changed in order to protect their privacy.

All rights reserved. No part of this book may be reproduced or utilised in any form or by any means, electronic or mechanical, including photocopying, recording or by any information storage and retrieval system, without permission in writing from Aurum Press Ltd.

A catalogue record for this book is available from the British Library.

ISBN-10: 1 84513 174 6
ISBN-13: 978 1 84513 174 6

10 9 8 7 6 5 4 3 2 1
2011 2010 2009 2008 2007

Designed in Helvetica and Garamond Simoncini
by Roger Hammond
Typeset by SX Composing DTP, Rayleigh, Essex
Printed and bound by CPD in Ebbw Vale, Wales

1

Who Killed Martin Hannett?

Martin might have bought the gun from any number of long-term, small-time petty criminals.

It is a neat Mauser, a German gun, with a long, phallic barrel. He had insisted on that. What's the point of threatening someone with a gun that hardly has a barrel? It's the barrel that gives the whole thing menace, meaning and authority. He wanted it to be German too, so that it had the total Second World War and Cold War resonance. He had considered buying a black leather trench coat to go with it; they are very popular right now in the late 1980s, but in the end he had decided against it. He might just look ridiculous, as if he'd come from a Second World War fancy dress party. Or, worse still, as though he was ironically referencing Nazi chic in the same way as Joy Division (whose name referred to the prostitutes who were available to the death camp commandants), or Siouxsie Sioux with her iconoclastic swastika armband.

He wants to be taken seriously. This is the entire point of the mission. A bullet in the right place is worth a million words, or something to that effect. He parks his car, now a battered old shit-brown Cavalier, just round the corner from Alan Erasmus's flat on Palatine Road, West Didsbury. It's over ten years since this was the venue for the camaraderie of packaging the *Factory Sample* extended player. It's nearly a decade since Ian Curtis hanged himself.

Thirty minutes ago he phoned Alan, one of the partners in Factory Records and Tony Wilson's right-hand man, to ascertain that Tony would be there. He recognises Tony's latest motor, some effete pale blue Renault. He yanks at the glove compartment. It doesn't immediately open. This will be bleeding great if he can't get the frigging shooter out. He tugs harder. A few courtesy CDs spill out. He doesn't like the CD format. It makes everything sound too clean and anaemic. There is no dirt or depth in music presently. The Giorgio Moroders and Trevor Horns have taken his own rhythmic doomy motorik and echoed vocals and turned it into vapid disco epics.

He finds the Mauser; it fits snugly into the palm of his hand, as advertised. This is the first time that he has held a handgun. He slips it into the roomy pocket of his overcoat. He looks more the part of the Oswald lone gunman than the fashionable politico terrorist.

It is drizzling.

Maybe he should find himself a grassy knoll and wait for Tony, then blow his head off from behind, as he drives off, in classic Dallas bookstore manner.

The cold steel in his hand does make him feel more potent. Conceivably a loaded gun can set you free.

He gets out of his shitty car. It embarrasses him. He embarrasses himself most of the time. He still hasn't allowed himself to feel the grief of his mother's death. He has been too numb and cauterised with drink and drugs and food. He is frightened of his own emotions. He feels that if he opens that can of worms, so many will crawl out that they might consume him, dead or alive. He has become a joke in the industry. The new breed of bands, the Madchester lads – the Happy Mondays, The Stone Roses, The High, the World of Twist, the New Fast Automatic Daffodils – recognise his ability and are graciously trying to bring him back out of the wilderness, but they gradually realise that he has become a liability and at most it ends up with a single or a couple of demos, before some dependable, day-job producer dude is brought in to rescue the sessions.

On the other side of the road a young couple are pushing a brightly coloured pushchair with an equally brightly coloured two-year-old, in OshKosh B'Gosh toddlers' togs, cooing and singing to itself. They are sharing a joke. They are laughing together. Both of their hands are on the handle of the buggy. The road rises with them. They have a future ahead of them.

He has a two-year-old son, James. He knows that he is incapable of providing the child with all the things that he is entitled to – warmth, security, food, encouragement, approval and love. He wants desperately to supply all those things and his inability to do so fills him with a sense of guilt and self-loathing that is so deep and toxic that no amount of drink, food, methadone, or alcohol can cauterise the fatal feelings. The drugs don't work.

So maybe he'll terminate Tony, spare Alan; then blow the top of his own swelling head off.

The downstairs communal blue door is open. It always is. He has no idea who lives in the flat downstairs. Does anyone know? Does Alan know? Is it the same tenant who has been there all those years and has seen Factory Records, Joy Division, New Order, World Domination and the Haçienda come and go? Possibly they have been totally oblivious to this slice of micro-history.

He rings the bell. Alan answers, as Martin knew he would. There are some patterns that never change.

'Hey Martin, my main man! Good to see you.'

Alan does his genial, black guy, soul brother greeting.

Martin nods. His teeth are clenched together. Some nu-dance shit is playing. It is the sort of spineless stuff that they pass off as trendy at the Haçienda Club, from which Martin is barred. By his own admission it upsets him so much that he is liable to become violent and deranged. Martin had wanted to spend some money on recording equipment, maybe a studio, rather than open a club for a bunch of minor megastars, witless wankers and arse-licking crawlers.

The woozies are still smoking dope for God's sake. Can't they handle proper drugs?

'Wrote for Luck' by the Happy Mondays comes on. Is this coincidence or planned? Is he meant to feel good about himself suddenly? He has produced the album – *Bummed* – from which it comes and some people have talked about a return to his old form, but he doesn't believe it and probably nor do they.

It is undoubtedly a blueprint masterpiece for the E and whizz generation. The lyrics, about the transient and unreliable nature of truth, are entirely appropriate. He has captured that hard, four to the floor, edge with them and then decorated it beautifully with all kinds of punctuations from horns and synths and quirky ambient washes. It hardens his resolve. The dubby outro fills the room. Shaun Ryder's voice dissolves into an almost childlike yodel, as the percussion track becomes more metallic and minimal. Tony is standing in the shadows. He is wearing a beige suit. Beige? For Christ's sake!

'Play it again Sam,' Martin demands levelly.

Tony produces one of his trademark smirks and hits the repeat button. Martin nods his head in rhythm to the irresistible percussive track.

Martin waits until the line about being clever.

'Do you reckon you're clever Tony?'

Martin's voice is still level, but there is a hard, murderous edge. Alan instinctively steps back. Tony foolishly comes forward. Martin moves a little to his left, blocking the exit. All these actions are syncopated perfectly to the instrumental break, the jabbing, stabbing horns.

'What is it that you want Martin?'

Tony betrays his impatience in his tone.

'Night Shift' by the Names, a track that Martin produced for Factory nearly ten years previously, but which now sounds puny and derivative, comes on.

'What is this Tony? Martin Hannett's Greatest Fucking Hits? Wouldn't you be better off waiting until I'm dead to release this lot? It worked with Ian, didn't it? Dead rock stars sell well. Turn it off, Alan. It's shit. It's all shit.'

Alan cuts the track dead.

All that you can hear is Martin's forty-fags-a-day wheeze.

'What is it that you want Martin?'

Tony uses his standby television presenter's technique – when in doubt, repeat the question.

'I want my money and my dignity back.'

He slowly raises his arm and reveals the gun, which he points directly between Mr Wilson's eyes. He notes the terror.

'Don't be so fucking stupid Martin.'

Tony tries to tough it out.

'Do you feel lucky punk?'

Alan attempts to stifle a chortle.

'Martin . . . Martin . . .'

Possibly for the first time ever Anthony H. Wilson is rendered speechless.

'Are you looking at me? ARE YOU LOOKING AT ME?'

Martin yells the line with such ferocious force that it threatens to tear his chest apart.

'Die then. Die you fucking twat!'

Martin pulls the trigger. Wilson staggers back instinctively. There is no retort, no loud explosion, no shower of skin and skull.

There is just a click. A dull click.

This incident – The Gun Incident – probably didn't happen. And at least it certainly didn't happen this way. Martin Hannett's legacy, apart from the extraordinary records he produced, is above all made up of myths. This is merely one of them. It was certainly controversial, and much disputed: did he, didn't he? Did it really happen? Was it loaded?

According to Tony Wilson it was based on another, equally unlikely, story about Martin shooting the receiver of his own telephone with a loaded gun whilst talking to Rob Gretton, New Order's manager, when, after Ian Curtis's death, they had been unimpressed with Martin's work on their first album as New Order and never worked with him again. (Allegedly, in fact, Martin shot his receiver twice. Presumably he either had two telephones, or bought himself a new one between incidents.)

And, also according to Tony, Martin *did* turn up at various times at various doors, late in the rain-drenched godless night. By then, he claims, the lawsuits and litigations were over and Martin had received a settlement that he had 'used up'. He says that Martin would sob and cry and ramble on about Ian Curtis's suicide and how he could and should have done more or said something. And then, according to Tony, he would shamble off out into the night, the rivulets of his tears mixing with the down-pouring of Manchester rain.

But the fact that the myth has gained currency tells us a lot about how people saw Martin Hannett. Pinning him down is like catching smoke. Extracting the myths from the legacy is next to impossible. Perhaps in the end we only have our own versions of the people we know. This, then, is my Martin Hannett.

2

Martin was born into a staunchly Catholic family on 31 May 1948 in north Manchester, and christened James Martin Hannett. He was the oldest of four siblings – one brother, Mike, and two sisters, Julie and Elizabeth. Martin had the oldest sibling syndrome. He tended to assume control; he supposed that he was cleverer than those around him. In his more tender moments he was capable of looking after younger people – thus his relationship with Ian Curtis of Joy Division. Julie had, however, always looked after him as a child, even though he was the eldest. He turned to the women in his life to nurse him, to tend and care for him.

They were a musical family – his sister Julie is now a cellist – probably through the influence of their mother, Veronica, who had grown up listening to big band music and jazz and swing. From an early age Martin had an obvious love affair with music and records, and would take a disc back to the record shop and demand another, because the first one 'didn't sound right'.

Their father had been a foreman fitter in a textiles firm and had spent a lot of his time abroad, fitting textile machines for foreigners and unwittingly contributing to the slow death of the mill towns in the North-West of England. Perhaps within this paternal scenario were sown the seeds of Martin's fascination with the whirring, grinding, clink and clank of heavy machinery and then the subsequent echoing, hollow silence when all that was left was vacant warehouses, voided factories and windswept front offices. For a time it seemed that Martin might follow in his footsteps, but the Factory he worked for would be a very different enterprise.

As a boy he would spend hours trying to create the perfect elixir. He was fascinated by the formula for Brompton's Cocktail, which in the past was given to patients with terminal diseases – equal parts alcohol, morphine and cocaine. He acquired a well-thumbed copy of MIMS, the directory of proscribed drugs, with its descriptions of medicinal compounds and the hidden properties of certain drugs. He would mix together warmed water, gin (pinched from his mother's drinks cabinet), Brut aftershave, Martini (shaken not stirred, obviously), lighter fluid, dab-it-off, Cinzano, essence of boot polish and anything else he could lay his hands on. He would mix and stir and heat and observe and test the results on himself. On occasion he made himself very ill, but it was all in the name of science and progress. A couple of times he started hallucinating – giant homicidal rabbits and mutating teddy bears – the usual thing.

Once or twice he got quite stoned and had to lie down and mumble incoherently to himself as the hazy images flickered in retinue behind his retina. On one occasion the concoction tasted very good and he drank several mouthfuls before he began to experience a burning sensation in the pit of his belly followed by dreadful flatulence and then severe vomiting and a blinding headache; he was convinced that he was going to die. But he found an antidote in the shape of a condensed-milk-based cocktail with castor sugar, syrup and saccharine. Thus began a lifetime's addiction to all things sugary.

He would learn mathematical equations and theorems and then test himself. He was drawn to quantum physics at a very tender age. He loved neat rows of digits and sines and cosines. He was always pleased by Factory Records' obsession with numbers and cataloguing. FAC 4 had a particularly pleasing symmetry: visually, phonetically and linguistically. There was always a hint of autism at play.

By his late teens he was one of a burgeoning number of youthful local musicians who had plenty of talent, energy and ideas but little creative outlet. He was a student at the University of Manchester Institute of Science and Technology (UMIST) in the late sixties, where he successfully completed a chemistry degree. His approach to music was influenced by his clear grasp and appreciation of chemistry, mathematics and physics. He understood the physical properties of sound; he was always fascinated by new technology. He knew that music and maths are the only 'pure languages' and from early on his interest in music was more technical, although he always maintained an inventive and experimental approach to production and recording. He was always keen to try something new and innovative. CP Lee, a one-time bandmate of Martin's, recalls him attempting to drive a beat-up old banger of a car into the sea at Southport beach. When he was asked why, he replied that he wanted to see what it would be like.

But it was as a fan that his enthusiasm was really ignited. He had seen every gig that it was possible to see in Manchester and its environs in the late 1960s – including the Beatles, the Rolling Stones, the Animals, the Yardbirds and Pink Floyd.

He attended many of these gigs with CP Lee, Bruce Mitchell and Les Pryor, who together with Martin formed themselves into a band in the shape of Greasy Bear. They played a stoned rock and blues repertoire; they had few ambitions for commercial success and they played together for fun rather than profit, for the friendship rather than any fame. They liked to jam. The name seemed to conjure up something big and furry and benign, but a little bit seedy, a bit greasy. They enjoyed it. The first gig, booked by Les, was at a gay club – The Penny Farthing Club. Martin played his bass on a camp stool with his back to the audience, ostensibly so he could better hear the foldback (the sound the musicians hear on stage) from the speakers, though according to CP Lee, there was possibly also a degree of pose involved.

The musicians shared various houses in Chorlton, south Manchester. Martin was living with Wendy 1 (as she would later become known to distinguish her from Wendy 2) at the time. He was something of a late developer when it came to girls. As a child and adolescent he had tended towards being overweight and self-conscious and to prefer the solitary pursuits of his chemistry set or reading or listening to his precious records to chasing girls. Like other similar, initially introverted, individuals, his charms didn't really reveal themselves until his teens when like a butterfly (and like Ian Curtis to some extent) he emerged, seemingly fully formed, with his dry wit, his easy charm and his knowledge of popular culture and music. He was hip and cool and knowledgeable; as such he became attractive to a particular kind of young woman who is impressed and fascinated by those qualities.

Wendy 1 was the first of these. She had been at university with Martin and according to CP Lee was 'an obscure object of desire' – all the boys fancied her from afar. She was skinny, beautiful and seemingly aloof. For three years they were inseparable, living together in a number of flats and shared houses in south Manchester – the student areas of West Didsbury, Fallowfield, Chorlton and Longsight – and admired and emulated as a 'cool couple'.

Martin, as a result of his diet and intake of amphetamines, had slimmed down drastically. He was of average height, about 5 foot, 10 inches in his woollen socks. His curly hair was usually an unkempt mess that would flower into an afro if left untended. His eyes were dark blue and warm and kind and could indeed sparkle. He had a great grin, a cheeky smile. He was a good-looking guy with an undeniable charm and unforced charisma; most women were instinctively drawn to him, and indeed many of them wanted to mother him. The dynamics of his relationships with men were entirely different and more complex.

It was a time when Martin was very much part of a 'gang', in stark contrast to how he would end up in the latter days of his life. There would be lively discussions after gigs about how the particular band had achieved their individual sound. Martin was particularly taken by a Bonnie Raitt gig whose bassist – Freebo – played a fretless bass, almost unheard of in those halcyon days. He was also intrigued by

Dave Edmunds, who as a producer was trying to replicate the Phil Spector Wall of Sound. There were huge quantities of dope being smoked, but dope tends to be a social drug connected with communal rituals, whereas heroin and its toxic cousins demand a more solo commitment and eventually alienate all friends and family.

It was at one of these gigs, whilst still a student, that he met Steve Hopkins. It was to be a turning point in his life.

3

Martin Hannett and Steve Hopkins met at a Soft Machine gig in UMIST Students' Union, circa 1971. Soft Machine at this time were very much a prog rock band. They boasted fine, experimental musicianship and a line-up that would go on to form and influence various bands for years, if not decades. At various times this line-up included such luminaries as Kevin Ayers, Robert Wyatt, Daevid Allen and Hugh Hopper, the bassist, a personal favourite of Martin's. They had evolved out of free-jazz doodling and stoned poetry happenings into one of the first underground rock acts. Their experimental approach and dislocated, spaced-out epics were to have a clear effect on the musical expeditions that Steve and Martin would later make under the anarcho-banner of The Invisible Girls.

Even if we weren't there, we can picture the scene.

On this particular night, in this particular place, there aren't that many people in the audience. Martin and Steve both have de rigueur shaggy long hair and equally shaggy long coats and they both nod and groove along to the numbers. The sound is loose, louche, sinister, including chunks of pre-recorded sound, and uses Stellavoxes and the Ferrograph, creating an avant garde, menacing, deep space symphony, with the vocals at times like ocean-deep narrations. This could well be the blueprint for Joy Division or The Durutti Column, once honed and stripped down and reduced to its lean fundamentals.

Steve Hopkins, who is also a student, studying maths and music, recognises Martin from the student fraternity.

Martin shakes a pre-rolled joint of Lebanese gold. He is chubby, his hair falling into his face and disguising the somewhat bloated visage.

'Do you play?' Martin enquires as they slouch towards the back of the hall, as the Machine's music continues to drift in an early version of ambient rock, or even drift rock itself (as embodied by new-millennium acts such as Labradford, Trans Am or the jazzier inflections of Tortoise).

'Piano, keyboards. I'm classically trained.'

There is no arrogance in this information; in fact Steve is an extremely modest and affable man. But Martin is impressed and intrigued.

'How about you?' Steve asks.

'I mess around with guitars. I'm partial to the bass.'

Steve likes him already. They discover that they have similar musical tastes. He recognises the young man's wit and intelligence. They both have a penchant for the more complex end of the progressive rock spectrum – thus their presence at a Soft Machine gig, a band that weren't exactly teeny-bop chart fodder. They realise that they were both at the Pink Floyd gig, recorded for posterity on the live album of the *Ummagumma* set, at Manchester College of Commerce. It had been a gig that had transformed Martin's perception of what one could do with sound, especially in a live context. In some ways it spoilt his appreciation of live music, which was less controlled and more problematic to carefully engineer than the studio environment wherein sound can be controlled and manipulated and shaped endlessly.

His ear, like Steve's, was always finely tuned and he found it difficult to accept music that was lazy, muddy or ill defined. He experienced punk as being limited in its insistence on the three-chord bash, paucity of musicality and suspicion of invention. In contrast he applauded the wild experiments of Frank Zappa, Captain Beefheart, Amon Düül and the more imaginative of the 'Krautrock' German bands.

By this time Greasy Bear are no longer functioning as a viable musical unit, if indeed they ever had. The various members' energies and time have become diverted elsewhere, although they will continue to operate more as a hobby for a while longer.

'Maybe we should do something together,' Martin suggests.

So, over the next twenty years Martin and Steve Hopkins do 'something together'. It is never anything as formal or formulaic as a 'band', but the two of them become a loose musical partnership under the banner of The Invisible Girls. As the name suggests, they are rarely seen, but provide the musical backdrop and compositions for a number of performers, especially the Bard of Salford, the People's Poet Laureate, John Cooper Clarke, who Martin will also go on to manage, chauffeur and make meals and strong tea for. Steve and Martin will create three albums' worth of original and inventive material with JCC for the major record label Epic. They will help kick-start his recording career with the *Innocents* EP on Rabid Records and along the way unleash a number of zany singles and extended players including the orange vinyl, triangular-shaped 'Gimmix' and the sublime 'Post War Glamour Girl', which Clarke himself described as 'a sure fire disco hit'. The recordings that Martin will help to generate as part of that ensemble will contain some of his most playful and creative work, not only as producer but as a musician. The music that he and Steve Hopkins will create as backdrops to Cooper Clarke's brilliant, witty and literate lyrics/poems will reference jazz, rock and roll, doo-wop, salsa, film soundtracks, blues, heavy metal, neo-classical, motorik, punk, Krautrock, BBC Radiophonic Workshop, frothy pop and more besides. The records will be opportunities for Martin, and Steve, to have fun and experiment.

The Invisible Girls will include a transient group of musicians, mainly from Manchester, whose number will include guitarist John Scott, drummer Paul Burgess, guitarist Lyn Oakey, Bill Nelson (on loan from his own Be-Bop Deluxe), Pete Shelley (on holiday from Buzzcocks), Vini Reilly (off duty from The Durutti Column), John

Maher (long vacation from Buzzcocks), Stephanie Formula on guest viola and Rob Blamire (Penetration).

And The Invisible Girls will become moreover the backing band for Pauline Murray, and provide a very modern, shiny and unexpectedly poppy backdrop to their own version of electro-disco or sci-fi dance on the *Pauline Murray and The Invisible Girls* album in October 1980, which will manage to dent the national charts at number 25. They will even go out on the road to back Pauline and John (the *Sounds* reviewer will write that Martin was 'seemingly making up guitar fills on the spot like a degenerate, chain-smoking Segovia'). And Martin will still be playing sitting down.

But back to the Soft Machine gig.

Martin spies a wooden bench at the back of the hall, so he and his new-found friend, and soon to be accomplice, settle themselves down.

'I'm going to lose some weight you know,' he informs Steve apropos of nothing, 'I'm only going to eat an apple and a cheese sarnie a day . . . and loads of amphetamines.'

That is exactly what he does: it keeps his weight down for the next ten years.

And for Steve the following years will become, as he puts it himself in 2005, 'The best of times and the worst of times.'

Soon after this gig Martin became part of the Students' Union Social Committee at UMIST, so he could book the bands that he wanted to see and hear and he was thus able to sample the shifting musical landscape of the period. His approach to music was always very British, perhaps influenced by the predominantly British bands that he saw at the time, but he also had a fondness for the more outré

American combos of the period. He had a particular affection for the charismatic Arthur Lee's Love. He gravitated towards powerful and doomed front men – Lee himself, Jim Morrison of The Doors and the mighty Jimi Hendrix. He went on to work with several powerful and opinionated vocalists – Ian Curtis, most obviously, and John Cooper Clarke but also Bono, Peter Perrett (The Only Ones), Richard Butler (The Psychedelic Furs), Shaun Ryder (Happy Mondays) and Howard Devoto (Magazine).

After having been named best student at Salford Tech (now University of Salford), Martin found himself a day job at Courtaulds, an engineering firm, as a laboratory technician. One could argue that he saw his role as a producer in not dissimilar terms. The recording studio was a sonic lab inside which he was the technician, the mad scientist and the mathematical magician. But he quit the job, grew his unruly hair longer and, as a result of the connections he had made as a booker, picked up casual labour in culture (Factory slogan) as a soundman and roadie. It was the classic apprenticeship, where he absorbed everything he could about the mechanics, practicalities and electronics of sound production, PA systems, amplifiers, speakers, bass bins, drum risers, hi-hats and gaffer tape. He fell out with his dad, who was not impressed by this career move. He had hoped that Martin might pursue a career in chemistry or engineering, and never really understood the long-haired, music-obsessed stoner that Martin became. From then on, they were not close, though Martin continued for a few years to come home to Miles Platting every Saturday, never on a Sunday, for a good lunch, hot bath and laundry. He avoided Sundays because the family went to Catholic mass, and Martin had very definitely lapsed.

4

In February 1973, Martin and some other cultural communists, anarcho-syndicalists, musical neo-Marxists and revisionist rocker Trots set themselves up in ramshackle offices in 100 Oxford Road, Manchester. This was Music Force, a Manchester musicians' collective, and as such a forerunner to the plethora of independent record labels and shops that would spring up around the UK in the mid- and late 1970s. The most long-lasting of these was Geoff Travis's Rough Trade in London. But others included Small Wonder, Fast, New Hormones, Stiff ('if it ain't stiff, it ain't worth a fuck') and Mute: the names alone conjured up heady images of speedy experimentation and rampant creativity. It was a time in British popular music when the rock dinosaurs of the early 1970s were gradually being replaced by the more youthful and energetic performers – Marc Bolan, Roxy Music, Sparks, Cockney Rebel and the godlike David Bowie – the spearheads of the glam rock movement that was to have such a (melo)dramatic effect on the advent of punk some three years later.

The building itself had once been a grand Georgian pile, but was now falling into rack and inevitable ruin. ('What is rack?' Martin would sometimes wonder out loud to no one in particular.) It was on the ground floor of this once splendid edifice that Martin had his office, as promoter, working amongst the piles of promotional posters, the ubiquitous flyers, the glue-encrusted buckets and their attendant industrial-sized brushes, all the tools of the flyposting trade, which would culminate in the fly-poster wars of the mid-1970s.

Here Martin was happy as the proverbial pig in shit. Indeed that was often how it felt. He took on the persona of the mogul, the rock entrepreneur, the music mafia man. He was full of vim, verve and vigour. He was rarely as happy, motivated and energetic again. This was his milieu. He could book bands. He was in control.

This is where we next find him, in conversation with Mick Middles:

'I promote a surly, incoherent mass of local talent which encompasses a huge spectrum of skills,' he explains to a youthful, fresh-faced Mick Middles, who is a cub reporter, looking for a good story, as all youthful, fresh-faced cub reporters do. Mick nods dutifully and takes notes, as Martin lights another cigarette from the stub of the previous one still smouldering in the overspilling ashtray, and answers another phone call with a mock-surly 'No, no, no. Impossible. Fuck off!'

'What were you saying?' Mick prompts politely.

'Any kind of music . . . within reason . . . another music from another kitchen . . . equipment hire, transport, support acts . . . you name it pal, we'll supply it. We do it all with a guerrilla consciousness and a peculiar nihilism reminiscent of a Japanese suicide squad.'

Perhaps this could describe Martin's approach to his work, and his modus operandi, for the next ten years; that and 'a certain disorder in the treble range', as he will explain to another fresh-faced journalist, Jon Savage, many years from now.

Martin swings his boots up onto the desk, folds his arms behind his head, and chews his cigarette as though it were an important cigar. He stares up at an imaginary fan that slices through the fetid air like the blades of a Hawk helicopter in that famous dissolve shot from *Apocalypse Now*. He hears those portentous, shifting chords from The Doors' dystopian epic 'The End'. It would be interesting to find a new Jim Morrison, he muses to himself: a boy with a big, bad, booming voice.

'I've always been a big fan of Revelations,' he tells Mick cheerily, without betraying his internal monologue, his obscure train of thought.

'Yes . . . some good writing in there, interesting images,' Mick concedes.

'Next question!' Martin snaps happily.

It is to his credit that Martin managed to adjust to the changes and moved with the mood and placed himself in a position where, according to one of his co-workers of the time, the entrepreneur and drummer Bruce Mitchell, he was 'relating to the next lot of musicians, which were the punk musicians'.

His life had changed too. His relationship with Wendy 1 had petered out some time before – they had drifted apart, and at about the time he became involved with Music Force he met Suzanne O'Hara, who was also promoting bands at the time. She already not only had a reputation for her startlingly beautiful looks, her good taste in music, her aura of mystery, her great taste in clothes, but also was seen as something of a muse for a number of local musicians. Like Wendy before her, all the boys desired Suzanne. She was of Irish descent and had incredibly piercing blue eyes, classic bone structure, long long legs and a model's figure. She could be volatile, but that is a trait that men adore in a woman. Suzanne was asthmatic and seemed to suffer from a number of illnesses. She often looked pale and wan. You wanted to protect her. She had a dry wit, like Martin. She is remembered for naming Sad Café – who were briefly fashionable just before the advent of punk.

She and Martin lived together for the best part of five years in their legendary flat in East Didsbury. (East Didsbury at the time was more fashionable and expensive and residential and upmarket than the more studenty West Didsbury.) She took to choosing Martin's clothes in an attempt to make him look 'trendier'. She initially went to local gigs with Martin but became more isolated as Martin's career seemed to progress. She was aware that she could be seen as Martin's girlfriend and wasn't happy with the Suzanne O'Hooligan nickname that was foisted upon her. She didn't want to be the Yoko to his Lennon, the Linda to his McCartney. But she struggled to find a niche and role of her own.

Suzanne was good friends with John Cooper Clarke, who would often crash at their flat, and provided him and other visiting musicians with endless tea and coffee and biscuits and comfort. She was a particular confidante and friend to a young Jon Savage, one of the best rock journalists of the time, who worked for the *NME* and later wrote, perhaps, the best book about punk – *England's Dreaming*. He was an early champion of Joy Division. Suzanne, too, knew quality when she saw it. She was appreciative of Martin's production work and had a fascination for the younger musicians that he worked with, especially the lads from Joy Division. She could be flirtatious and seemed to be flattered by their attention and admiration. She had a particular soft spot for Jilted John aka Manchester Polytechnic drama student Graham Fellows. She was quite often, literally, surrounded by men. Years later when she booked bands for the Beach Club, she was able to get the 'guys' to do more or less anything for her. She was a good listener and had several male gay friends who liked to confide in her.

But by early 1977 Music Force was a spent force; it had run its course and Martin and Tosh Ryan moved into an old grocery shop at 20 Cotton Lane, Withington, Manchester where they formed Rabid Records, and Martin was able to fulfil his dream of setting up a recording studio. Tosh, even then, seemed considerably older and more experienced than everyone else on the scene. His background was in earlier Manchester music scenes – jazz and blues. He was a dyed-in-the-wool socialist, perhaps even an old-school communist, but an entrepreneur too. He was the founding energy of both Rabid Records and Music Force, both of which he saw as having a political agenda and structure.

For Martin too it was also a business opportunity. His first productions included recording incidental music for the politically motivated Belt and Braces Roadshow, one of a growing number of leftist theatre companies that included the feminist collective Monstrous Regiment, the Scottish 7:84, North West Spanner, Red Ladder and the first all-male, all-gay theatre company, Gay Sweatshop. The dividing lines between theatre and music, between fine art and commercial design, were being blurred. The cultural cross pollination had begun. There was energy, excitement, rebellion, revolt in the air.

Martin produced and promoted a Nigerian band from Stoke-on-Trent, called Afro Express. He discovered how the mechanics of record distribution worked, from initial concept through record pressing and packaging to final product. He understood the means of production and thus, in a Marxist sense, was empowered. And throughout this he still found time to collaborate with his friends and peers Bruce Mitchell and CP Lee in Greasy Bear, by now on a very occasional, ad hoc, just-for-the-fun basis.

His biggest move at the time, and perhaps a career-defining moment, came when he worked with one of Manchester's, and indeed Britain's, finest punk rock bands – the Buzzcocks. He already knew them from having booked them a few times through Music Force. Howard Devoto, who was their lead singer and lyricist at that moment, gave a pragmatic reason for using Hannett's skills: 'Martin was the only person we knew in Manchester that was known as, or called themselves, a producer'. From such stuff are legends born.

The four tracks that comprised the *Spiral Scratch* extended player were all recorded in a speed jive eight-hour session at Indigo Sound Studio on 28 December 1976: literally on the dawn of Punk Year Zero – 1977. It was the no man's land between Boxing Day and New Year's Eve. It was, perhaps, a cheap time to record, as the post-Christmas days were a 'down period', but Martin liked to operate in no man's lands, in uncharted territory. In those early days he was adept, fresh from his guerrilla experiences with Music Force, at organising time, space and even budgets. Part of a producer's function, like a theatre director, is to make sure that everything happens when it is meant to happen, that the cast are where they are meant to be, that they have rehearsed and know their lines, that they are protected from the outside world as much as is possible whilst engaged in the holy act of creation. Martin was as pragmatic and practical as was required. It was only later that he began to run over schedules and budgets in his obsessive search for the perfect beat or the ideal rim shot or the next hit. Steve Hopkins remembers him as being 'very organised and efficient . . . able to bring the best musicians in when necessary . . . right up until the third [John Cooper Clarke] album'. He also recalls that Martin was usually able to go back to whatever record company was footing the bill and prise a further 50% beyond the budget, by a mixture of charm, guile, sheer insistence and determination.

Spiral Scratch was groundbreaking in a number of ways. It was only the third UK punk record, after The Damned's 'New Rose' and the Sex Pistols' 'Anarchy in the UK'. It was the first to be produced outside of London. It was the first independent release on Richard Boon's New Hormones label, with the sexy catalogue number ORG 1. It contained four tracks – 'Breakdown', 'Friends of Mine', 'Time's Up' and probably the best-remembered, most-loved and frequently referenced track – 'Boredom'. It sold an incredible 16,000 copies, mainly by word of mouth, before being re-pressed and reissued. It is full of raw primal energy and adrenalin, but it is still very much a work of art. The key track 'Boredom' not only expresses that terrible sense of emptiness, futility and frustration through the title, the lyrics, the sneering voice, but even in the legendary, faux-dumb, two-note, Pete Shelley guitar solo. It was brave of Martin to use a two-note guitar break in the middle of 'Boredom'. As CP Lee describes it in *Shake, Rattle and Rain*,

'The break consists of the same two note pattern repeated frantically over and over again, 66 times before slithering off into a final modulated seventh that leads back into the chord structure.' It is a fine example of the medium being the message, and the message being the medium, or in this case, the tedium.

On the back of the original sleeve were printed all the recording details, equipment used, overdubs employed, in an attempt to demystify the process of production, very much in a Marxist dialectical materialist deconstruction. This was music that by its very presence and existence was challenging and seditionary. It opened the door for thousands of young hopefuls and the formation of hundreds of 'indie labels' and their various anarchic ideologies. This felt like the time when the workers could take over the factory and the means of production and produce wonderful objets d'art rather than dull, perishable consumer goods. Martin was certainly aware of the irony of this, having come from a background that was inextricably linked, economically and sociopolitically, to mills, factories, cheap labour and mass production.

This era was the start of the strained relationship between the independent labels and the majors, which would be a part of the creative tension within the popular music scene for the next few years. The indies seemed to do the groundwork, to nurture the bands at the early points of their careers, as they were struggling to find their musical feet, before the Big Boys with their cheque books and extravagant promises would sweep in and sign them up to terrible contracts. Some independent labels, more cynically, sold their bands on to major labels, or reached some kind of fairly lucrative licensing deal with them. But it was an uneasy marriage that would inevitably end in a messy divorce.

Martin gave the *Spiral Scratch* tracks the slightest suggestion of ambience. He somehow managed to make the sound feel concrete.

Musically it was a break from the hegemony of the previous years (the early and mid-1970s) and the reign of the Guitar Rock Gods – Eric Clapton, Jeff Beck, Jimmy Page and Jimi Hendrix.

Martin was on a roll. Whilst still involved with Rabid Records he worked with the Wythenshawe glam punk rockers, the boot boy punks, Slaughter and the Dogs, on their foaming-at-the-mouth, barking-mad ode to speed, 'Cranked Up Really High'. It was appropriate: this was the time when copious amounts of amphetamine sulphate were fuelling the new punked-up, white riot explosion.

But he also found time to work with the much mellower Chris Sievey and his Freshies on their more poppy, new wave outings. Chris Sievey generously described Martin as 'my favourite person to work with in the whole world'. He worked with the criminally undervalued local singer-songwriter Pete Farrow on six tracks, within which he managed to make Pete's acoustic guitar sound massive and to capture the eccentric essence of the seemingly simple songs. There was little or no financial remuneration involved and Martin did it out of fondness and appreciation for Farrow and his idiosyncratic talent.

He crammed in sessions with Ed Banger and the Nosebleeds (within whose riotous ranks was Vini Reilly, soon to be an integral part of The Durutti Column), Gyro and a Manchester Polytechnic drama student called Graham Fellows who as his alter ego Jilted John created the faux-dumb, novelty hit classic 'Jilted John', with its memorable chorus of 'Gordon is a moron'. It managed to hit number 3 on the pop charts. Martin helped Jilted John to cobble together a cash-in album entitled *True Love Stories*, which was released on EMI. CP Lee reckons that some of Martin's most imaginative and playful production and compositional work appeared on this now almost totally overlooked platter.

5

At the same time as working with the rabid young pretenders, Martin began his much longer-lasting, adult relationship with Salford poet John Cooper Clarke. It would endure through the creation of three albums, various singles and EPs, television appearances (on *The Old Grey Whistle Test*) and even a national tour.

They had first met after Tosh Ryan had bumped into Clarke, perhaps literally, on the street. John was dressed up as a giant rabbit. To this day no one knows why he was thus attired, but he referenced the experience in a later lyric in 'Post War Glamour Girl'. They had first rubbed shoulders as early as 1972 when Music Force was promoting gigs, initially at Houndsworth Hall in Deansgate, central Manchester. Martin performed at an event there himself, playing bass guitar as part of Greasy Bear. John and other Zen-like and eccentric characters performed their poetry and performance art around the outskirts of the hall.

Later on, in the punk and post-punk era, JCC would often open the evening's entertainment with a rapid-fire performance of his incredibly witty, surreal, hipster lyrics. He needed no backing band or equipment: just Johnny Clarke and a mic. He was often part of the same bill as Buzzcocks and Joy Division. The Southerners didn't seem to appreciate him or his Northern wit.

John had been born in Salford and was christened the Bard of Salford by his devoted, though small, brigade of fans, but has always been wilfully obscure about his background. He told tales of giant rabbits and UFOs to explain his birth, as well as referring to 'having been born outside the womb'(sic).

Apparently he had lived in a beatnik house for many years with an old hipster poet (and many cats, though whether feline or as in the 'hep cat' sense was also unclear), who he had then based his persona on. But this could be an entirely apocryphal story, designed to throw the newshounds off his trail. John and Martin liked to invent stories about

'Cooper Clarke' as they sat in Martin's kitchen getting steadily more strange. At various times they imagined that he had been an awful orphan, an only twin (in a nod to Peter Cook), a foundling (found in a basket in the Manchester Ship Canal) or one of his poems bizarrely come to life.

He and Martin shared a fierce intelligence and a surreal sense of humour and a deep appreciation of the absurd. Martin 'got' John and vice versa. John wore shades, because his eyes looked 'dreadful and would scare small children' – the same reason that Roy Orbison did.

Their first work together was on the *Innocents* EP with its blatant, deconstructed use of the drum machine ('we all start when the drum machine starts lads') coupled with distorted guitars, boisterous bass and peripheral, unsettling sound effects and that 'certain disorder in the treble range', which Martin himself reckoned was part of his trademark, distinguishing sound. It is present in most of his productions and subliminally provides a disturbing experience for the listener. It sounds as though something is sonically 'wrong'. It is in contrast to the much 'cleaner' sounds achieved by producers whose sensibility is arguably more 'pop'. While Nick Lowe, for example, who worked with Elvis Costello on most of his early albums, as well as producing his own witty and eclectic output, was able to rename his albums for the lucrative American market, so that *Jesus of Cool* became *Pure Pop for Now People*, Martin's productions never really made it across the Atlantic. They retained a much 'dirtier' feel. He was starting to develop the separation between individual instruments that would become another signature. He would explore the whole range from rumbling, sonorous bass to tinny treble overload and everything in between.

The first full album that John Cooper Clarke and Martin worked on together was the fabulous *Disguise in Love*, released in 1978. It became the blueprint for their combined approach, and was an inspired meeting between Clarke's rapid-fire, literate, witty lyrics and Hannett

& Hopkins's playful, inventive, imaginative musical backing. Martin even revisited the stripped-down guitar solo from Buzzcocks' 'Boredom', but this time on just one note during the break in 'Post War Glamour Girl'. Legend has it that it took eight hours to perfect and record.

It is with Cooper Clarke and Hopkins and the other Invisible Girls that Martin can be heard at his most relaxed, joyful and accomplished, both as producer and musician, best evidenced on their magnum opus 'Beasley Street', which builds from a faux-funk shuffle to an urgent discoid symphony with ambient sweeps, swoops and leaps, behind John's brilliant description of a north Manchester street and the state of the (dis)United Kingdom in 1978. It captures the sound and smell, fear and feel of north Manchester in the late 1970s better than any other recording.

Martin was John's manager, chauffeur, gofer, confidant and friend for a number of years. It was the little-seen side of Martin that was supportive, encouraging and selfless. CP Lee observed that they shared a common interest from '*The Beano* to Einstein'. They had the same sense of humour and would go happily in search of the sound of silence on Saddleworth Moor together, if Martin felt it was necessary.

Picture this . . .

Martin, John Cooper Clarke and Steve Hopkins are loaded up with substantial recording equipment that they have borrowed, via the broadcaster Mr Anthony Wilson, from Granada Television Studios. Clarke and Hannett are climbing up a steep incline on Saddleworth Moor, the killing fields, the charnel ground, of that infamous Manchester duo Brady and Hindley. Steve as always manages to look dapper and handsome and from a different age. There is always an air of academia about him – old world charm. Martin wearing his afghan coat, which he has swathed himself in for a number of years, a long scarf tied around his neck, old blue jeans tucked into boots. John looking totally incongruous, given the outdoor surroundings, in a skintight second-hand Oxfam suit, the sleeves way too short, his hair more of a meltdown mess than even Martin's, dark glasses as ever shading his eyes from the world and the world from his eyes.

Martin is carrying a big old furry microphone – the fur prevents howl-round – on a boom. It's a shame nothing has been invented to prevent howl-round in the head. John is lugging a reel-to-reel recorder on his slim shoulders. It is possibly a Revox, the professional's choice of the period, but it could be an Akai, Ampex, Concorde, Dokorder, Ferrograph (unlikely, too antiquated), Nakamichi, Panasonic, Reflectograph, Sansui, Stellavox, Tascam, Teac or an Uher. The names themselves are resonant and reverberate down the sonic ages. This is still the age of splicing: audio can be edited as a physical presence, usually by the professional, at an angle. This appeals to the physicist in Martin. It speaks to the boy within who had loved to take transistors apart, or to experiment with early tape recorders such as the German magnetophones. He had created sonic collages, in the style of Cage and Stockhausen, from found sound, random radio bursts, chiming clocks, rudimentary percussion, static, disembodied voices from the monochrome (television) set, mother's music boxes with their twirling prima ballerinas. These were his palettes and paints, his oil and gouache, his paper and pens.

John is woefully ill attired for this expedition, for although it looks like an idyllic spring day, we know how quickly the climate can change on the Moors, from mild to wild, from balmy to barmy, in the space of minutes. The fog can descend and make visibility zero. Just like the fog that would descend on Martin and rendered him invisible, many years later. If only he had invested in some howl-round.

But, for the pleasant present, they are making their way to a grotto, which Steve Hopkins has found, within which the acoustics are fantastic. Martin is keen on recording in unusual ambient spaces, be they grottos, caverns, grotty outside toilets, lifts, cliffs, phone boxes and, infamously and unfortunately for Stephen Morris, benighted drummer for Joy Division, the studio's granite roof for several chilly hours.

He wants to record 'some silence'. They wander, happy as clouds, trying to locate the grotto, which by now is being referred to as 'the grotty' in cod Scouse accents.

'I am certain it was round here somewhere,' says Steve.

Martin and John collapse in a fit of giggles and become snarled up in the recording equipment.

'I can hear the breeze Martin,' John says through his laughter. 'Do we need any breeze? We could . . . shoot it.'

Martin lies on his back watching lonely Lancashire clouds scud across uncharacteristically blue skies.

'I think I can hear the sound of grass growing,' he informs them, paraphrasing lyrics from The Move's psychedelic pop song.

'You need to call the fire brigade, man,' Cooper Clarke ripostes, in the same vein.

They have their own rapid-fire lingo. They have an implicit understanding and respect for each other that extends into the work they do in the studio. It is seldom, if ever, discussed.

'There it is! There it is!' Steve shouts, gleefully pointing at some boulders.

They pick up their equipment and walk.

'It's just a bunch of stones, Steve,' Martin remarks with good humour.

'I think the cave is under the stones. If you roll them away,' Steve suggests seriously.

'Maybe you should record them then, Martin. Maybe you should record the Stones – the Rolling Stones!'

And the three of them fall around in a further attack of absolute jollity and delight.

'Let's record the Stones, then,' Martin states flatly. 'Let us record the Rolling Stones – their Satanic Majesties near to these Satanic Hills . . . and let us build . . . Jerusalem . . . in England's green and pleasant land.'

He continues, gazing out boldly, one arm mock-heroically across his chest, across the windswept hillocks.

'Yeah, but we all know that England's dreaming . . .' John drawls, imitating the Rotten snarl perfectly.

The three of them fall about joyfully again.

6

Soon after the day out on the Moors, Martin was wooed and courted by Tony Wilson (whose day job was still as a presenter of *So It Goes* and the local news at Granada Television Studios) for the nascent Factory Records label. It had been Tony's ultimate dream, and one that he realised through force of will, hubris, bravado and sheer personality, to have his own record label. Factory Records was formed at exactly the right place, at exactly the right time. In 1975 England had been not only dreaming, but was possibly comatose. The economy was in recession, unemployment was at an all-time high. There was no future, or so it seemed.

Musically the mid-seventies were the time of the dinosaur bands, perhaps exemplified by Led Zeppelin, Rory Gallagher, Black Sabbath and Deep Purple with their ponderous heavy riffing, guitar hero antics, stadium anthems, twenty-minute drum solos, bared torsos, fringed jackets and white boy cosmic blues. They were the New Gods from afar, on High. It would soon turn into the worrying genre of prog rock as demonstrated by Soft Machine, King Crimson and Yes (with their triple albums such as *Tales from Topographic Oceans*) and Pink Floyd's 'trippy' *Dark Side of the Moon*. It was dopey dope music to be listened to on 'the cans, man'.

The recreational drugs that were favoured were cannabis resin, Californian grass, Mandrax and (Stateside) Quaaludes. It was downer music for downer kids and their older hirsute siblings. But the seed change had commenced with glam rock – David Bowie being the prince whilst the courtiers included Marc Bolan, The Sweet, Cockney Rebel and even early Slade. In their own realm existed the heavenly Roxy Music and across the pond were Iggy Pop and Lou Reed and the New York Dolls.

The musical *The Rocky Horror Show*, soon followed by *The Rocky Horror Picture Show*, with its gender-bending, retro rock and roll, sleazy decadence and trash aesthetic would also be a big influence, as was the cinematic version of *Cabaret* with a young, divine Liza Minnelli as a debauched, yet innocent Sally Bowles and Joel Grey as the androgynous, menacing Master of Ceremonies.

But in 1976 things began to change and initially the change came, unexpectedly, from Bromley, Kent in the 'Sarf' of England. This was the stomping ground of the Bromley Contingent, who included Siouxsie Sioux, Steve Severin and Jordan and who soon joined up with the arty World's End Clique, with their headquarters in the sex shop, top of the King's Road in Chelsea, London, who numbered Malcolm McLaren, Vivienne Westwood, and very soon Johnny Rotten and the other Sex Pistols, in their ranking ranks. It was time for the new punks in their new boots and panties.

The musical antecedents had been laid by pub rock bands like Kilburn and the High Roads, Brinsley Schwarz, the very influential Graham Parker and The Rumour and the magnificent Dr Feelgood. Indeed, another pub rock combo – Eddie and the Hot Rods – would release one of the first punky and adrenalin/speed-fuelled paeans to the new freedom in the shape of 'Do Anything You Wanna Do'. Out of London and its environs came a slew of anarchic acts – The Clash, The Stranglers, The Adverts, Ian Dury and the Blockheads, Wreckless Eric, Rachel Sweet and Elvis Costello, hosted by their very own independent labels such as Stiff, Rough Trade and Chiswick. And the Sex Pistols themselves.

In his fabulous book about the Manchester music scene (1955–95) CP Lee heads one of his chapters with the title 'The Anti-Christ comes to Manchester'. It describes the first visit of the Sex Pistols to the Lesser Free Trade Hall on Friday 4 June 1976, which he compares to Dylan's visit to the same city in 1966, a mere decade previously – so much can change in ten years.

Actually there were two Sex Pistols gigs at the Lesser Free Trade Hall, but most people either only remember, or were only present at, one and in most minds the gigs have become conflated, if not confused.

The legendary gig was on Friday 4 June 1976. From this seismic event, attended by a mere 70 punters (although nearer 7,000 would claim to have been there), came the burgeoning of the Manchester punk and new wave scene with its own Northern take and slant on the energy and anarchy of its Southern (some might say idiot) cousins. The audience included a whole host of future illuminati – present, amongst others, were Ian Curtis and fiancée Debbie, Peter Hook, Bernard Sumner, Tony Wilson, Stephen Morrissey, Howard Devoto, Pete Shelley and Martin Hannett, soon to become Martin Zero, as everyone needed a punk moniker in '76. (Step up Rat Scabies, Joe Strummer, Poly Styrene, Dee Generate, Captain Sensible, Sid Vicious, Gaye Advert, TV Smith et al.) Out of this congregation would arise Buzzcocks (who in the form of Devoto and Shelley were the promoters of the night, as well as being the support band), Joy Division, The Smiths, New Hormones and Factory Records. It was a weird collection of early punks, old hippies, Pips kids, Bowie boys, Siouxsie sisters, local eccentrics, Manchester Polytechnic students, lefties, Dave the Dealer, John the Postman and odd-bods. Some were still in old flares, some had converted to the soon to be de rigueur drainpipes. Leather jackets made an early showing, but so did fringed jackets and even afghan coats. Hair varied from newly cropped and spiky to long and shaggy. There were winkle pickers and brothel creepers, and sadly sandals too.

Malcolm McLaren, the Pistols' manager and man who, according to himself, single-handedly invented punk rock, stood outside the venue like a street hawker trying to drum up trade. 'Step right this way! Anarchy in the UK! Come and get your punk rock. This is the way, step inside!'

Admission was 50 (new) pence.

The Pistols were in blistering, blitzkrieg bop form and tore through a set that included some of their own compositions and some apposite covers. They opened with their own 'Satellite', which accurately captures the boredom of living in a New Town – think early Milton Keynes. Glen Matlock was on bass in those early days, not yet replaced by Sid Vicious. Matlock could actually play the bass guitar and the growling bass sound pinned the whole thing down and gave it a menacing and sinister feel. Likewise Steve Jones on guitar and Paul Cook on drums knew their primitive rock chops. But it was Johnny Rotten's snarl and sneer and leer and bent-over shapes that captured the imagination as he spat, hissed and phlegmed his way through their brutalist repertoire.

Martin Hannett would have been struck by Matlock's bass playing, as he stood, near to the front, hair obscuring his face, Suzanne O'Hara at his side. In the film *24 Hour Party People* Martin is seen pogoing frantically to the Pistols. It seems highly unlikely that he would have pogoed as he had a deep resistance to dancing or indeed any form of physical exertion. His tendency was to stand still and very slightly nod his tousled head to the uber rhythm, sometimes smiling mysteriously to himself. He would eventually be scathing about the punk rockers, accusing them of being revisionist, conservative and lacking in imagination. Martin was a musician. They, on the whole, were not. He once referred to punk rock as being 'R & B on speed'.

In their set they performed a riotous version of the Monkees' ('I'm Not Your) Steppin' Stone' and The Who's 'Substitute' – in many ways The Who, along with The Kinks, were one of the proto-punk bands. The Pistols' own numbers included 'Lazy Sod', 'Pushing and Shoving' and they closed with 'Pretty Vacant', wherein Rotten draws out the vowels so it becomes 'vaaa-cunt'.

A member of the audience taunted Rotten with 'You're a wanker', another shouted 'This is bollocks' – perhaps providing the Pistols with the title for their first album *Never Mind the Bollocks*, which in turn would give Nirvana their album title *Nevermind*. The sound and statement of intent were clear, the aggression and energy were palpable and the small crowd went crazy.

The Pistols returned, just over a month later. By then word had spread as had drainpipe jeans, ripped leather jackets and spiky hair.

And, like many others, Tony Wilson was inspired. And his inspiration would lead to Factory Records. Of course he was aware of what Martin Hannett and Tosh Ryan were doing with Rabid Records and certainly he had heard and been impressed by Martin's incredible work with Buzzcocks on the sensational *Spiral Scratch* EP. It could be said that he 'poached' Martin from Rabid to Factory.

Tony, in his book *24 Hour Party People*, recalled meeting Martin on the Moors at midnight, a rather Shakespearean conceit. Martin was wondering 'what sound would be like if it had to travel through a completely different atmosphere, through strange weather and weird gravity'. It was perhaps a train of thought that led, many years later, to the sound of the Joy Division song 'Atmosphere', whose sonic texture is exactly that. His Pink Floyd UFO mystical roots were showing: he wanted 'to hear the sound of the moon moving around the Earth'. It is all part of the 'Mad Martin' myth.

So Martin moved from Rabid to Factory, from mad dogs to Cool Designer Englishmen, and became part of the Factory 'board' that at the time comprised self-styled media mogul Tony Wilson, jobbing actor Alan Erasmus and designer Peter Saville. Later it would include Rob Gretton, manager of Joy Division, once JD became the best commercial bet and it was easier to have the manager on the board. But it was always a loose conglomerate. There were few, if any, contracts and most things seemed to be done in a fairly arbitrary manner. This modus operandi would later be the cause of much friction between Martin and his 'partners', when he felt, rightly or wrongly, that he had been cheated out of thousands of pounds and the rest of the 'directors' chose to build the Haçienda Club rather than invest in studio and equipment.

Factory Records was named not after Andy Warhol's Factory, as is often assumed, but supposedly after a sign that Erasmus saw near to the Russell Club that read 'Factory Sale'. It was a word that was incredibly resonant in the North-West of England with its history of mills, chest complaints and an impoverished population of factory (and cannon) fodder. It had an austerity that was soon reflected in Saville's post-industrial designs: neat, clean neo-classical lines, reliance on silver, grey and black and the use of industrial symbols. The working man with the protective earphones that featured on the posters and records was an apposite emblem. One of the things that drew many people to Factory Records and their eclectic output was the 'look'. It was slightly detached, and entirely different from anything else that was happening, in design terms, at the time. After the cut and paste and rip it up and start again and Xerox and splatter gun approach of punk, it was quite a surprise.

Martin said at the time that he was going to be 'Head of A & R (artist and repertoire) and production'. It is a moot point as to whether he was ever 'head' of anything. Tony always remained the chief executive. It was his game, his baby.

The relationship between Martin and Tony was probably always an uneasy, amorphous one that was lacking in any real cohesion or shared vision. They were, however, perhaps more similar than maybe either of them would admit. They were both grammar school Catholic boys. They both had an enthusiasm for and faith in the power of popular music. They had both started off by grooving to the mellower tones of progressive rock, and in Tony's case West Coast AOR soft rock – The Flying Burrito Brothers, Andrew Gold, Emmylou Harris, Neil Young and eventually the ubiquitous Eagles. They were both older, and maybe wiser, than the young protégés and angelic upstarts who they championed and recorded and marketed. They both had an academic approach to their chosen milieu, although neither of them would have characterised it as such. They enjoyed their motor cars – Tony favoured French automobiles, Martin was enamoured with the Swedish marques. They both had a fondness for slim, willowy women.

But Tony always retained the veneer of a hip businessman, an alternative entrepreneur (in the mould of Richard Branson or Brian Epstein). Tony was a groovy uncle; Martin was a grouchy older brother. Tony had the day job at Granada Television in central Manchester. He had the house in Cheshire and the wife – Lindsay Reade at that time. Martin was beginning to make his way, but never shrugged off the stoned, outsider, maverick persona. He was never a team player or a corporate man (however alternative the corporation might have seemed). He had the flat in Didsbury and the gorgeous girlfriend – Suzanne O'Hara by this time – but he never had a career or really a public profile. Tony was pretty straight. Martin always had a propensity for the darker stuff, and the obsessive nature of the diehard addict. Martin was a Marlboro man; Tony had a love affair with Gitanes and Gauloises.

Tony and Martin weren't known to socialise together, although at the start they would attend the same gigs. But as time went on Martin attended fewer and fewer live gigs. He preferred to stay in and listen to records on whatever state-of-the-art equipment he had most recently acquired. He claimed to never really enjoy playing live himself – perhaps the reason why he played sitting down, sometimes turned away from the eyes of the audience. He was, essentially, a private man, whereas Tony thrived in the public arena – he was and is a Media Man.

Tony saw his role as bringing together individual talents who could work together and create something extraordinary and magical and creating environments – whether in studios, venues or clubs (most famously the Haçienda) – where amazing things could occur. In some ways he was a patron of the (popular) arts. At other times he could be the Svengali, the puppet master, but he would usually graciously accept the autonomy of his mannequins. But Martin was never easy with the role, or even the suggestion, of being a manipulated puppet. Although he produced all of Joy Division's recorded output for Factory Records and other Factory bands as well – A Certain Ratio, Section 25 and the Names – he was as, if not more, interested in the world beyond the Factory. His work with John Cooper Clarke was for the far more formidable Epic Records and he laboured for CBS and EMI and saw himself very much as sonic gun for hire: the lone arranger.

Tony and Martin both needed others to realise their dreams and ambitions and even to provide a voice for their thoughts, ideals and fears. They would both, in different ways, find that voice, that mouthpiece, in the slender, epileptic frame of Ian Curtis, on whose slim shoulders they rested the weight of their worlds.

Where it all started was at the Russell Club in deepest Hulme. Hulme was a sixties architect's insanity, a grim folly, with blocks of flats built in circles facing in on each other. It rapidly became a dystopian no-go area, habituated by petty (vacant) criminals, drug dealers, gangs of disaffected youths and impoverished and demoralised families. The Russell Club was an unprepossessing-looking building with a fairly nondescript front and had been a reggae and blues club and home to some of the West Indian community from nearby Moss Side. The owner was Don Tonay.

Inside, the club was larger than you might have imagined and the stage was of generous dimensions for a live club, with a good deal of depth. There were even rudimentary dressing rooms backstage. The downstairs had an empty dance floor, where the punters later would pogo and pose. At the back, facing the stage, ran the long bar, well stocked with extra-strong lager, and Julie's Burger Bar, which served a mixture of hamburgers and sausages and sometimes Jamaican cooking. There was always something burning. Ladies and Gents toilets were right beside the entrance and were surprisingly clean and hygienic. Stairs at the far side led up to a balcony, and further steps to a smaller bar, which was carpeted. This upstairs area became an ad hoc VIP zone where the cognoscenti and the shakers and movers and those in the know would gather and gossip and make deals and deal drugs to each other. There was usually the familiar aroma of ganja wafting through the building. The mixing desk for live bands with the turntable for records was downstairs, although sometimes it would be moved upstairs if the visiting band had a bigger rig or fancy lights and strobes that they hoped to dazzle the assembled throng with. It had atmosphere to spare and for a brief period was the only place in Manchester to play and to be seen at.

It was at an audition at the Russell Club that I first met Martin Hannett.

It is late November, 1978. Tony has decided that as Factory is a record label, it would be a good idea to release some records, financed by a small inheritance that has recently come his way. He has a band, The Durutti Column, who have done a couple of gigs at the Russell Club, as part of the first 'Factory nights'. They are Tony's pet project, but they have recently fallen apart. A succession of singers has either been sacked or left and now the rhythm section of Tony Bowers (bass) and Chris Joyce (drums) has jumped ship to form Mothmen and eventually will become Mick Hucknall's rhythm section in Simply Red. (Mick at the time was fronting the frankly ludicrous punk band Frantic Elevators.) I am here to audition for the part of lead vocalist.

I am already a big fan of Martin's recorded output and own most of the artefacts with which he has been involved up until this point. I am especially taken with the *Innocents* EP. What has impressed me is the sheer wit and intelligence that has obviously been at work in all areas of the extended player – the lyrics, the packaging, the musicianship and above all the production, courtesy of Martin Zero, as he is now styling himself. He is moving things along from the straitjacket of three-chords bash-street punk to something much more exciting and creative – post-punk.

I have been working as a jobbing actor in repertory theatres as glamorous as Derby Playhouse, as well as doing 'bits' at Granada Television – *Fallen Hero*, *Crown Court* and *Coronation Street* (in the epic episodes when the Rovers Return has been reduced to rubble by a collision with a passing juggernaut and the entire nation fears that little Tracy is trapped, or even dead, under the fallen masonry. I have the immortal lines, just before the iconic theme tune, 'They've found something sir.' And the whole nation collectively holds its breath, hearts stop beating, blood ceases to pump. 'Looks like a kiddie's doll.'). At Yorkshire TV, all the way up in Leeds, I have appeared in *Second Chance* and *Midnight Caller*. I have cornered the admittedly small North-West England television market in punky types and have already appeared with green hair as a punk photographer and bright red hair as a new wave deejay. It might be as a result of this that I have caught the attention of Tony Wilson, or it could be that his partner in crimes, Alan Erasmus, also a jobbing actor based in the North-West, has heard mention of me. Alan's current girlfriend, Anne, is mates with my current girlfriend, Louise. I am also a regular ligger at all the right gigs from those at The Squat to Pips to Rafters and beyond. I am one of the first (comparatively) Young Men to chop my hair into a punky mess, wear make-up, a dog collar (literally), drainpipe jeans, Doc Martens and the regulation black leather biker jacket (as a result of this look I have already been attacked by Teddy boys, threatened by skinheads and insulted by authentic bikers). I am thus attired for my audition as singer for The Durutti Column.

The only other people in the club are Alan Erasmus, who has kindly picked me up from my home in Withington and driven me over in one of Mr Wilson's cars; Tony, in a tasty, and tasteful, dark blue suit on his lunch break from Granada Studios, just round the corner; Dave Rowbotham, rhythm guitarist with what remains of The Durutti Column; and slumped at a table all on his lonesome, looking cold, grumpy and dishevelled, the Man himself, Mr Martin Hannett.

I recognise Tony from Joy Division and John Cooper Clarke gigs at the Band on the Wall. I assume that Dave is with the band as he has a Les Paul slung around his slender shoulders and looks every fucked-up inch the punky rock 'n' rebel that he always wanted to be. His hair is jet black and sticks out in several directions. He has the pinched, Dickensian, street urchin look of the undernourished and unloved. Less than twenty years later his head will be cleaved apart by an unknown attacker.

'Colin, hi!' Tony shakes my hand, always the media guy, always the Charming Man. 'I hope you don't mind doing this. We need a vocalist. Our previous one was a prat.'

'A twat,' Dave Rowbotham corrects him from the deserted stage where he is plugging his lead into his amp.

'Well, perhaps that's unfair,' Tony ameliorates, 'but we've had a parting of the ways.'

'A parting of the red fucking sea.'

I peer into the dimmer recess of the club and the table where Martin is sitting. He is smoking a cigarette. A Marlboro: my brand. The drug addict's brand. The only cigarette you can really taste when you're whacked out. The taste of the Big Sleep. Martin by this point is starting to dabble heavily in narcotics, although he always maintains that he can control it, he can deal with it. His fingers are interlinked and folded under his chin. His hair is a mass of dark curls. He is wearing a dark green cardigan. Our eyes meet across what will soon be the legendary venue. At this moment in time, it has been host to a few Factory nights, but mainly is known as a downbeat reggae club, the haunt of Black Guys and White Whores, like the shebeens/blues clubs in Bradford that I frequented when I was doing an acting stint there. This is one of the reasons for the unlikely alliance of dub and punk that Martin will pick up on and later incorporate so well into his oeuvre with outfits like Basement 5 and A Certain Ratio. As always, there are practical reasons for these collisions.

Martin nods at me. We have similar leanings and fascinations – intellectual, revolutionary, visionary, music-obsessed, culturally conscious, fingers on the Zeitgeist.

The performer in me takes over. I climb onto the stage. After all I'm the guy who sang 'Ziggy Stardust' in its entirety, drunk on a half-bottle of whisky and a handful of blues, for an audition for *Jesus Christ Superstar*. Someone has set up a Shure mic on an old stand, gaffer tape holding the whole thing together. It's plugged into the guitar amp.

'What do you want to do Col?' Dave asks me.

I sense the amphetamine sulphate coming over him in waves. It connects with the speed in me.

We do the Velvet Underground, of course.

The Velvet Underground will always be the touchstone, the starting point, the common denominator for those who really understand. It is no coincidence that Martin worked on a wonderful version of 'All Tomorrow's Parties', in 1982, with Nico (originally ice maiden chanteuse with the Velvets) and the Invisible Girls or that Joy Division did a cover of 'Sister Ray', or that Orchestral Manoeuvres in the Dark, who Martin also produced, did a take on 'I'm Waiting for the Man'.

We decide on 'Sweet Jane'.

Behind the heavy shades he has put on we are watched by Martin 'Zero' Hannett. I already own everything that he has so far produced. I am first, foremost and for ever, a FAN.

It is nerve-wracking. But we launch into it nonetheless.

I play it lazy and throwaway and louche for the first couplet; then I go for the fashionable sneer. I vamp up the streetwise lyrics.

Martin leans forward a fraction. The boy looked at Johnny.

Dave speeds it up a touch for the next few lines, then we both instinctively lean in together for the ultimate chorus . . .

Martin stands up and yells with us, or maybe at us.

'Sweet fucking Jane!'

Dave steps back from the mic stand, winks at me, grins goofily, exposing broken, stumpy teeth.

'You got the gig man, you got the gig.'

Martin sits back down, lights another Marlboro straight from the previous one and nods at Alan Erasmus, who nods back, Mr Tony Wilson turns and catches the tacit agreement and nods to himself: all done on the nod and it's a done deal. I have impressed Martin Hannett, and Tony Wilson and Alan Erasmus have always acknowledged that Martin is the sounding board. He is the one with his ear to the ground. He is the guy who understands the gestalt. He knows where it has come from and where it is going to.

He is The Man.

7

A couple of days after my audition Alan Erasmus dropped round to my house with a cassette, recorded on which were two instrumental tracks. He didn't sit down or stop – he was always on the move, moving something (equipment, furniture, Peter Saville-designed 12-inch singles) or someone (Ian Curtis, Jilted John, Linder from Ludus) from A to B.

The point of *A Factory Sample*, as the title would suggest, was to present various Factory or Factory-influenced bands – namely Joy Division, The Durutti Column, Cabaret Voltaire (from Sheffield) and the alternative comedian John Dowie. It was hoped that it would herald the existence of Factory Records to an eager, but still slightly comatose, public. It was also conceived as a work of art and subversion. It was full of Situationist slogans and images, although rather obtuse and vague. It was subtitled 'Labours in Culture'. There were four sides, called Aside, Beside, Seaside and Decide. The bands featured were chosen by Tony – as well as managing The Durutti Column he was enamoured with Joy Division and friends with 'the Cabs', who had already played at the Russell on a number of occasions. It was felt that it would be good to leaven the proceedings with some comedy, thus the odd presence of Dowie, a kind of Northern Alexei Sayle for the punk generation. The sound would be eclectic, surprising, challenging, uncomfortable, experimental and represent a departure point for any intrepid fellow travellers. It achieved all those things and more, easily selling out its initial pressings and becoming a real collector's item and an object of astonishing beauty, thanks to Peter Saville's gorgeous designs.

The two Durutti instrumental tracks had been previously laid down by the band, which comprised Vini Reilly on lead guitar, Dave Rowbotham on rhythm guitar, Tony Bowers on bass and Chris Joyce on drums.

It was these tracks that were presented to me by Alan Erasmus.

'Tony said – could you put some words to these?'

The given titles are 'No Communication' and 'Thin Ice (Detail)'.

'Right . . . OK. I'll try.'

'Fine. And I'll pick you up tomorrow morning.'

'Tomorrow morning?'

'To go to Rochdale.'

I suddenly feel like a proper rock star that has appointments made and minders to look after his emaciated frame and his every winsome whim.

As agreed, Alan calls round for me at precisely ten past eleven. He knocks three times on the front window. Overnight, I have listened to the two trax (rock and roll spelling) several times in a diligent manner and have scribbled some possible lyrics for each 'piece' on the backs of old brown envelopes. I hunch my leather jacket on, stuff brown envelopes into one pocket, felt-tipped cassette into the other, make sure that carefully wrapped gram of sulphate is secure in zipped top pocket.

'Yeah, I'm ready Eddie.'

'I'm Alan,' Erasmus deadpans back as we head for Tony Wilson's waiting, engine running, light blue Volvo.

I sit in the back with Tony. He is very much the Manager, although uncertain, at this juncture, whose image to adopt – a toss-up between Joe Meek, Andrew Loog Oldham, Brian Epstein or Malcolm McLaren. Eventually, in true magpie fashion, he will filch elements from all the above and create his own hybrid.

'What have you got Col?'

I am unsure whether he means my literary efforts or any Class B drugs I might have secreted about my person. I cover all eventualities by producing my envelopes and patting my left-hand top pocket to let him know I'm sorted for whizz. He takes the envelopes from me with due care and attention. Alan is driving alarmingly fast. Wilson scans my words, as he will some early evening news copy just before talking direct to camera.

'These are good. I like these. Would you mind if I added some stuff?'

He produces a red felt-tip pen and for a terrible moment I fear that he is going to cross out my efforts, but rather he writes a couple of lines, on one side, with a veritable flourish and then hands it back to me.

The lines read 'Keep the traffic moving' (we have stopped at some traffic lights), 'Travel for pleasure alone' (we are having fun, but a clever ambiguity: does he mean alone in the sense of by oneself, or for the sole purpose of pleasure?). Then an obscure, somewhat abstract line: 'Liquid stockings, repairable but stolen', though it may be that I have just misread his sloping, ornate handwriting.

'See if you can scan those in.'

So I do. I scan them right in there.

A seeming matter of minutes later Alan deposits his passengers outside Cargo Studios, in Rochdale. Like most locations in this saga, the studios are freezing fucking cold: brass monkeys, as the Mancs would have it. Dave Rowbotham is there, strapped into his guitar. I don't remember ever seeing him without his guitar, or attendant strap, but I imagine he wasn't wearing it when he was axed to death. Then again . . .

'All right cock?'

This is the first time we've seen each other since the bootleg Russell Club audition sessions. I suddenly feel vulnerable and insecure and therefore in need of some chemical input.

'That's right, you two have met,' Tony remarks.

'Sweet Jane we have,' Dave concurs. Like Martin, he likes to reinvent language. Like Martin, he will eventually take it too far.

On cue Martin appears. With him, looking rather nervous and out of place, but very handsome, is Stephen Hopkins. He is never really at ease with rock and rollers, always more of a classical musician and a back-room boffin at heart.

'So you're the new singer,' Martin states, hinting at a long line of previous singers.

'Something like that,' I mumble.

Actually, I am overcome by the reality of meeting The Great Man properly for the first time. I want to tell him how monumental *Spiral Scratch* sounds, how much I dig the distorted, dirty guitar sound on *Innocents*, how divine the double-tracked bass on 'Sleepwalk', from Cooper Clarke's debut album, sounds.

He saves me: 'Have you got any speed?'

'Yes, as it happens, I do.'

We cram into the booth. The walls are carpeted – a cheap way to soundproof. There are a couple of no-nonsense engineer-type blokes fussing with fuses, plugs, echo chambers, wire, perhaps even primitive delay units.

Several wraps of amphetamine sulphate are produced and opened out like fortune cookies. Martin chops them out with an embryonic credit card into several lazy zigzag lines. He goes first, hoovers up a long line.

'Kinnel Tommy, that's rough,' is his verdict.

Dave and I, representing the new punks on the concrete block, are obliged to do two. Eyes water, mouths instantly dry. The engineer-type blokes shake their heads, not in any judgemental way, but they have practical stuff to do and pints of ale to be quaffed at lunchtime.

'OK, we all start when the drum machine starts lads,' Martin quotes the spoken intro to John Cooper Clarke's 'Suspended Sentence'. For a moment I take him literally and panic because there was no drum machine on the tape – was I supplied with the wrong tracks? – but the speed kicks in, my scalp crawls, I get the reference and I'm ready for any-fucking-thing.

Martin swivels on the chair and surveys the 'desk'. This is his toy shop, his domain and his kingdom. He places his three packets of Marlboro and his Zippo lighter on his left. He runs his right hand, palm downwards, over the knobs, faders, indicators – the controls. This is his ritual. He is the Shaman; he is setting the controls for the heart of the sun. He is in his time capsule. He is far removed from the quotidian struggle.

'Right then, what have we got?'

He pushes himself away from the control desk and looks up at Tony Wilson who is hovering around like a spare part in a spare part shop. Tony liked to be present, at least to begin with, at all stages of the process. He is fascinated by the means of production. Martin, for his part, sees him as getting in the way in his sacred studios.

'So we're just going to bang some vocals on the top, add a bit of keyboard colour, some sonic texture, then see what kind of cake that makes.'

'You're the producer. You're the Magician,' Tony accedes graciously.

Martin considers this, but doesn't comment. Tony often variously describes Martin as 'the Magician', 'a nutty professor', 'Gandalf of the poppy' (with fine double meaning), or 'a music fiend'. Eventually Martin will come to resent what he sees as the implicit patronising tone in such descriptions. He doesn't want to be the nutty professor in Tony's toy set who can be brought out and moved around and played with and then put away safely in a bottom drawer.

At this stage, Tony is still in awe of the production work that Martin has done only a few weeks previously, in the same environs, with the Joy Division lads. Two tracks of awesome power and fractured splendour in the shape of 'Digital' and 'Glass' that will be their contribution, and the main selling point, for the planned *Factory Sample*. Martin has taken the raw material provided by Ian Curtis and the boys and transformed it into a jagged aural landscape.

'That speed is bloody marvellous,' he comments, employing one of his character voices from his repertoire. He was always a great mimic.

'He seems like a nice kid,' Tony agrees.

'If his vocals are half as good as his chemicals . . .' Martin adds.

Then he leans into the linking microphone.

'Do you want to hear the first track again, our kid?'

'That would be handy,' I deadpan back.

Then the maelstrom kicks in, the mammoth, clattering drums and the portentous dubbed-out bass and the Neanderthal hum of some terrible dread. This is the filthy symphony that Martin has concocted with the dirty Durutti boys and then mixed on his own into something monstrous and massive. Martin has the line switched on so that when I start to intone . . .

'Dance . . . to the Disco Radio . . .'

. . . he can capture that spontaneous performance. He knows that vocalists cannot resist rehearsing, can't resist listening to the foldback of their own voices. And he is absolutely certain that the first take is invariably the best; the first cut is the deepest. I am in my cathartic capsule. Martin is my pilot. He sets the dials for the dark side of the moon, with his co-pilot ever vigilant, watching the meters and meteorites. Martin understands the paradox of the vocalist – the vanity and the insecurity. We are linked by the wires and terminals and a silver astral thread. We are terminally wired, totally wired. I provide the words and the voice. He gives it space, spontaneity, depth, width, atmosphere. This is his magic.

We complete the take of 'No Communication', with spoken word passages, devilish vocal effects, space rock middle eight, knowing nods to krautrockers Can, dub wizard Lee Perry and Syd Barrett-era Pink Floyd. But the whole heady witches' brew sounds totally fresh and original and he has indeed captured the spontaneity of a near-live vocal performance, seamlessly welded it onto, and stitched it into, an existing backing track. He has worked his Hannett hoodoo voodoo. His mojo has been working overtime, and his six senses. He beams at me: it's a Hannett moment. You want to please the man – another trick of the great producer. You crave his approbation. He has that effect on those that come near him. Even after his death, far more people will claim to have been his friend, his dealer, his gofer, than could possibly have been the case. He has a great smile.

We have made something together. The alchemy has worked. I glide back through to the control room. I am walking on amphetamine air.

'Shouldn't that be "dance"?' Tony asks.

He uses the Northern 'a' sound, the shorter vowel sound rather than the elongated Southern and/or posh pronunciation. Muso scholars will be discussing and arguing this point for years to come. Should singers vocalise in their own authentic accents or should they appropriate the transatlantic nu-speak that was so popular in the 1950s and 60s and even into the early 1970s? Punk took everyone hostage and insisted on working-class credibility and angels with dirty faces and Doc Martens inverted snobbery, and it was considered de rigueur to come from some broken home, to be in possession of council estate, tower block, Westway credentials. Admitting to being middle class was tantamount to punkoid career suicide, or even suicide itself. Some 'punks' went as far as reinventing themselves and having a revisionist attitude towards their own personal histories. Of course the irony was that the main movers and shakers in the whole scam were, as always, middle-class ex-art school, drama conservatoire types like Malcolm McLaren, Vivienne Westwood, Julien Temple, Peter Saville et al. It had been the same in the 1960s with Andrew Oldham, Brian Epstein and George Martin.

'What? You what?' Martin snaps back at Tone.

'It sounds a bit Southern and poncey,' Tony retorts.

There is always that tension between the two business partners. Tony wants to be the artistic director, the creative consultant in the Factory firm. Martin never kowtows to Wilson, or indeed to anyone. Tony is also suffering from the Northern prejudice that claims that anything that isn't Northern is poncey, pansy, poofterish and lacking in gritty authenticity. The dynamic between them has always been based on friction and an implicit power struggle.

'A bit Southern and poncey,' Martin sends him up, giving him a taste of his own medicine.

'Just my opinion.'

'Aye. Well eh up me lad, as long as there's no trouble at t'mill.'

He punches a few buttons on the console to bring up the final moments of 'No Communication', now with added-strength vocals, and slams it up so we all hear my voice booming and exhorting and eternally echoed with that long 'ah' sound. 'Daaaance!'

'Nowt wrong with that our kid. You take my point Tony?' Martin gibes.

'No, but you're the Magician,' Tony appeases tactfully.

'I'm not the Magician. Jesus effing Christ! Where do you get that idea? I'm just a geezer Tone. "I'm not Jesus, I'm just a fella,"' he quotes from *Whistle Down the Wind*.

Tony walks away, in tetchy silence.

'Let's have a wee break and then have a bash at t'other one, eh Col?'

Martin is on a roll, he is in his element, his natural habitat. He is the heavyweight music champion of the world. His word goes.

'OK,' I agree, uncertain of the protocol. 'I need some water.'

'Anything what your heart desires. Minion, fetch the singer a quaff of H too Oh! Ah, no minions. But there's a tap in the bogs!'

'The Gentlemen's toilets are outside, round the back of the shack,' Tony says neutrally.

'The Back of the Shack? Good name for an ACR album Anthony.'

They're mates again. We are all one.

'You got any more of that dynamite speed Col? It's outrageously nutritious,' Martin enquires.

I hand him my depleted wrap.

'That was bloody good mind,' Dave Rowbotham offers, appearing from nowhere, guitar welded to his waist, the picture of the low-down dirty junkie rhythm guitar slinger. 'I need a slash; I'll show you where the bogs are.'

It's not totally clear whether the bloody good refers to the speed or the vocal performance.

'Don't worry about Tony and Mart; they're always barracking each other. Martin is my main man, mind. He always will be.' Dave grins and leers at me. I sense that he imagines a future for himself with this down-sized version of Durutti. We zip up and nip back up some imaginary, or real, stairs. Dave punches the stagnant air.

'Aw fook,' he yowls.

He grasps his cranium in both hands and staggers back into me, almost knocking me back down the steps.

'What is it man? What the hell is it?'

'It's probably just some crappy shit what they put in that speed. I'll be all right, Jack. Never worry about me.'

'That stuff is the best. It should be pure. It shouldn't be cut with anything,' I try and reassure him.

'It's all cut, cock. Nothing is pure. Nothing is as it seems.' His eyes are red from the sudden agony. He rubs them harshly with his balled-up fists. 'Martin is a great guy you know. He's a big man. He's got a big heart, big ideas . . . I tell you what . . . he's Mister Fookin' Big.'

It's like a manic Manc version of the Dennis Hopper photojournalist character in *Apocalypse Now*. Dave chuckles filthily and the moment of pre-emptive agony has passed.

Back in the relative security of the studio we get ready to do the vocals for 'Thin Ice (Detail)', to give it its full, arty-pretensions title. The track swirls in like mist on that blasted Scottish heath. It comes in like a wave of phase. Then it lazily settles, Vini's guitar arpeggios swarm around as something more bass-inclined roots it down and I start to intone.

Martin is sliding faders up and fading sliders down and doing all kinds of studio trickery and the cursed Cowboy Dave is leaning into the non-existent wind, looking for shelter from the storm and even Mr Anthony H. Wilson is captivated for a fleeting instant.

After a lengthy spoken prelude, an anti-pop agit-prop prologue, the rhythm appears for the first time, and the bass starts a propulsive riff, the sense of forward motion that Martin is such a master of, and the drums hint at militarism and the vocals pick up on the propulsion and slyly suggest a minimal melody. Then the double-tracked, incandescent, individualist guitars break out free of their constraints. We dance on the graves of the deathly dictators and bloody bureaucrats and lifeless lackeys. We celebrate our energy, our lovely libidos, our collective subconscious (sic) and then the track jives out and off in pure rock and roll merriment, taking us back to innocence and another kind of Eden.

Martin Hannett shouts with glee: 'By fucking George, he's got it!'

It's a great view when you're standing on top of a mountain; but it's a long fucking way down.

Alan Erasmus, the quiet one, is sometimes remembered, unfairly, as being the gofer/chauffeur, but it was his famous flat in Palatine Road that saw the start of Factory Records' forays into the public domain. It was there that the Joy Division boys, and anyone who dropped by, were given jobs in the packaging of the elaborate *A Factory Sample* silver and black gatefold sleeve. There was a sense of camaraderie and excitement as they laboured over the beautiful, but ridiculously elaborate, Saville sleeve. They joked and joshed and carried on like boys do.

Saville himself had been a Manchester Poly art student and was renowned for missing deadlines, once turning up with a poster for a Factory night at the Russell Club days after the gig had happened. He was a mercurial, slightly aloof and charismatic character, but the look and style that he produced defined Factory visually and conceptually. He wasn't too bothered with, or interested in, the music, though he was a confirmed Roxy Music fanatic and finally got to design their sleeves too.

Alan was always polite, thoughtful and considerate. It was Alan who brought round £200 for me, in a pink plastic wallet, as payment for my vocal efforts on the Durutti tracks. It was Alan who would ferry musicians to and from gigs. It was Alan who could provide comfort and consoling words. At the time he was indispensable to Tony. It was in fact Alan who had come up with the name Factory Records.

A Factory Sample saw the start of the Factory empire and some diehard JD fans reckon that the JD tracks – especially 'Digital' – represent them at their most powerful, energetic and groundbreaking. Likewise Martin's production work on both the Durutti and JD numbers is seen as a quantum leap in his career. This was the point where he began to mix dub, punk, ambient, electronics, rock and roll and sound FX into a fantastic and frightening new concoction: the Brompton's Cocktail of the new wave. It provided a blueprint not only for JD, but a whole slew of new acts. The *Sample* initially sold 10,000 copies, almost entirely by word of mouth, and was praised in the music press by Morley and Savage and the other hip young journo guns. From then on people sat up and took notice – including the London crowd. It defined the difference between Northern and Southern post-punk, because it included wit, comedy, authenticity and artistry, without ever taking itself too seriously.

8

Having recorded with Martin, however briefly, I began to hang out with him. We discovered that we had a common interest in Class A drugs. Most people that we knew were still smoking some dope, taking a fair amount of amphetamine sulphate and maybe the odd line of cocaine. But using narcotics set you apart from the post-punk pack. It was a secret society, often shunned by our contemporaries. Class A drugs were far less prominent in those days and were frowned upon by our peers. It was an exclusive little club that we were members of. It had its own strict door policy and secret code of behaviour. It was more difficult to join than you might imagine. Martin's attitude to drugs and the rock and roll lifestyle was always ambivalent. He never considered himself part of the whole over-the-top rock and roll circus/pantomime. In fact his attitude could be aloof bordering on contemptuous. His drug use was done mainly at home, by himself, or in the company of close associates. He saw his drug use initially as a creative tool and a form of extreme experimentalism, even a form of spiritual research, and he was sure he could stay on top of it, but there is an old Chinese proverb – for the word 'drink', substitute 'drug' –

The man takes a drink
The drink takes a drink
The drink takes the man.

And there is another truism, which is 'One is too many, a thousand never enough . . .'

It is 1979, in the late spring/early summer.

Martin collects me from my house in a state of barely contained glee. He is the big kid who has just received the bestest present ever in the whole wide world. He won't tell me what the excitement is about and there is no music playing on the in-car stereo as we make the swift trip.

I follow him up to his sitting room. He has prepared everything. Two huge pieces of best kitchen tin foil with two of the thickest, most generous and darkest brown lines of scag on them that I have ever been privileged to see. There are Pioneer household matches, the extra-long safety sort. There is a jug of iced fresh orange juice and two sparkling tumblers. All that's missing is balloons.

'Do you want to hear this?'

He has, in his hands, the impenetrable black acetate of *Unknown Pleasures* by Joy Division.

We chase some serious dragon. I lie on the floor. He puts the black vinyl on, then sits curled up on an armchair in his trademark dark green jumper.

I am captivated, captured and catapulted from the opening propulsive rhythmic bars of 'Disorder' with its snaking guitar lines, sinuous bass pattern and Ian's sweet, doomed voice. I lie there transported and transfixed. Some of it is so dark and resonant and beautiful that it physically hurts. It works in a visceral way, involving all the senses, the sixth included. I don't break the spell, not even for another chase. Martin watches my reaction. He is utterly alive and alert. This is his child meeting another human being for the first time.

I absorb the agonies of 'Day of the Lords', the luminosity of 'New Dawn Fades', the neurosis of 'She's Lost Control', all the way through to the redemptive, glass-breaking catharsis of 'I Remember Nothing'.

What he has done is create such a sense of space and at the same time such a specific sense of place that you feel as though you are at times inside and at other times outside the music and that the music is within and without you. At moments you are in some cavernous underworld, the next in a dungeon, then trapped within a metal box, then stranded in your own cranium. The sound of the album is centred on the combination of the vocal and snare drum treatment. Stylistically, and in some ways thematically, it is reminiscent of *The Idiot* by Iggy Pop combined with the minimalist motorik of Neu!. Of course it owes a huge debt, indirectly, to Bowie's masterpiece of alienation *Low*. It is highly theatrical. Instinctively Martin has understood Ian's pressures and personal demons and has built the soundscape around that. It tells a story, however lateral and abstract. It is the ancient journey of the soul seeking salvation.

Ian Curtis was born into a working-class family on 15 July 1956 in Old Trafford, Manchester. His sister Carole was born four years later. He enjoyed school and attended Sunday School. (Martin and Ian both had an understanding of faith and the power of religion and religious symbolism that would surface in their work.) Ian got into grammar school (King's Grammar, Macclesfield). He was fascinated by history – especially the history of the Wild West and Native Americans, Richard the Lionheart and the Crusades. There was an incident when Ian and another boy sniffed cleaning fluid and took some pills and Ian ended up having his stomach pumped. After he left school he got a job in the Civil Service. He loved football – according to his family he was a Manchester City rather than a Manchester United fan. Sport in the seventies was definitely considered 'unhip' amongst the hip crowd, and Martin, certainly, had no interest in it at all.

Music was Ian's first love, though. He had formed his first band – Treacle Teapot – when he was 12, and in his early teens he became interested in David Bowie – eventually to the point of obsession – and Lou Reed. Like Martin, he was an avid gig goer, although he was attending gigs in the early 70s, rather than the late 60s. His formative period was the glam era – Roxy Music, Cockney Rebel – all of whom he saw live, a lot of them at Manchester's Hardrock venue. On the night of his first date with Debbie Woodruff he saw Bowie in his Ziggy

Stardust incarnation. He was 16; she was 15, also from Macclesfield. He became a 'Bowie boy'. They saw the film *Cabaret*, with its depiction of Berlin decadence and the rise of the Nazis, a dozen times. He saw Lou Reed on his Rock and Roll Animal Tour, in which he reworked such Velvet Underground classics as 'Heroin', 'Sweet Jane' and 'I'm Waiting for the Man'. This was the Lou Reed persona – cropped bleach-white hair, skeletal features, alienating the audience, aura of addiction, evil and debauchery – that was to have such a profound effect on the glam boys and glitter girls who would spearhead the punk explosion a mere three years later. This imagery also heralded the start of a dangerous flirtation with Nazi chic and the theatre of cruelty. It was a period in popular music that Martin would later admit had passed him by at the time, as he was still enjoying the headier, cerebral delights of progressive rock. It was a crucial, but potentially creative, difference between them, which would comc together in the creation of *Unknown Pleasures* and later *Closer*. That was the meeting of the Bowie boy and the prog rock hippy.

The glam gang tanked up on pills and cider, speed and cheap wine; the proggers liked their dope, man, for which they were eventually derided by the new punk kids as they started kicking over the traces. In the prescient words of David Bowie's 'All the Young Dudes' – 'my brother's at home with his Beatles and his Stones, he never got off on that revolution stuff: speed jive, don't want to be alive when you're over 25'. Martin could well have been the brother at home with his Beatles and his Stones, although Martin *did* get off on that revolution stuff and the speed jive, and had the savvy and the good taste to move and groove with the (post-punk) times.

Ian left the Civil Service to take up a job behind the counter in Manchester's vinyl emporium Rare Records, where he was happily surrounded by obscure 45s and import albums. It was a stopping-off point for the local music obsessives and fledgling punk rockers, many of whom would go on to form the key Manchester bands of the late seventies – The Fall, Buzzcocks, Frantic Elevators, Magazine, The Drones, V2, The Smiths. Ian was working alongside guys who were a little older than him, highly educated in all things musical, laid back and usually long-haired. This could have been a prototype of his relationship with Martin. Ian had great respect for the music cognoscenti, of which Martin was undoubtedly one.

He had a spell trying to sell his own stock of albums at Butter Lane Antique Market in central Manchester and although in business terms it was not a success it afforded him further opportunities to hang out with people on 'the scene' and talk about forming bands. But the record-selling business wasn't providing Ian with a living, and he returned to the Civil Service. By April 1974 he had become engaged to Debbie; they were married the following year on 23 August, still both in their late teens.

Ian began to frequent Pips, or Pips Disco, to give it its full title, which was fast becoming an unlikely spiritual home to the Bowie boys and proto-Siouxsie girls and Roxy rakes and Bryan Ferry clones who would include Peter Saville, myself, Stephen Morrissey, Peter Hook and Bernard Sumner. Pips started 'Bowie nights' – where the soundtrack was exclusively Roxy Music, David Bowie, Lou Reed, Iggy Pop and a smattering of European sounds, especially the hugely influential Kraftwerk. With their pioneering use of synthesisers and their creation of the whole autobahn motorik shtick and Man Machine ambience they were to become a blueprint for Joy Division and Martin's work with them.

You wouldn't have bumped into Martin Hannett at a Bowie night: at the time he was hatching plans with Tosh Ryan to start Rabid Records (home, in the end, to some of the rougher glam lads such as Mick Rossi of Slaughter and the Dogs). Suzanne O'Hara did pop in a few times with her flame-red hair and her exciting blue leather jacket and skintight jeans and cheeks like geometry and all the young dudes fell at her stiletto feet.

This was the melting pot that would give birth to early Manchester punk: a meeting of glitter and Salford grit. Amphetamine sulphate was beginning to put in frequent, cheap appearances, as it had done already on the earlier Northern Soul scene at Wigan's Casino, Manchester's Twisted Wheel and numerous other Northern clubs. In some, the management turned off the taps in the toilets and charged for a glass of water as they realised that speed made you very thirsty indeed.

Another common reference point for the young pretenders was the mid-seventies disco sounds to be found on a Sunday night at the University of Manchester's Student Union. There were records by Johnny Bristol, Kool and the Gang, Labelle, Rufus, Barry White, Minnie Ripperton. This would provide the more dancey element for some of the emerging bands. The Manchester bands always had that backbone of rhythm – just listen to Joy Division's 'She's Lost Control' or 'Transmission' or to Magazine's cover of Sly Stone's 'Thank You (Falettinme Be Mice Elf Agin)' or any number of the backing tracks on the John Cooper Clarke albums. The ping of the syndrum, the snap of the snare drum and the chug of the rhythm guitars were borrowed and revamped and revitalised.

Whether Ian and Martin were aware of each other's presence at the seminal event that was the Sex Pistols gig is unclear, but such are the subliminal strands and psychogeographical threads that invisibly tie our lives together. Often it is only in retrospect that a pattern can be discerned. At the time: stuff just happens.

Shortly after the Sex Pistols gig, a slew of new bands was formed and 'punk' gigs became a more common occurrence at venues such as The Electric Circus, the Ranch Bar and ultimately Rafters and the Russell Club, championed by music journalists like Paul Morley, Jon Savage, Ian Wood and Mick Middles.

Soon the Band on the Wall in Swan Street, which had been more of a sedate jazz and blues club, similar to Dingwalls in London, began to host its own punk nights. It was there that Martin, and Suzanne, regularly saw Ian Curtis perform as part of Joy Division, after they had metamorphosed from Stiff Kittens to Warsaw and then finally emerged in their final line-up.

The Band on the Wall was aptly named: the band playing were literally positioned in front of a brick wall, no elevated stage, no fuss, no nonsense, with a minimal back line of amplifiers and speakers, and a rudimentary house PA system. The audience squeezed themselves between tables, or stood on chairs at the back, and the other walls appeared to sweat and the floor vibrated. But it was a great testing ground for new acts and for a while Joy Division seemed to become the house band.

The musicianship was fairly basic, and the song structures unformed, but the mesmerising point was the intense young man in the middle at the microphone, his eyes often closed, stick-thin, usually clad in grey, utterly absorbed in the agonies and revelations of his lyrics. His surprisingly deep baritone seemed to come from somewhere else and there were the beginnings of his odd, insectlike, spasmodic trance dance. His arms would jerk, his elbows would pump up and down, his hands would dance under his elbows.

Martin stood and watched him and made the connection to other rock shamans like Jim Morrison and Mick Jagger and Arthur Lee. He noted too the raw potential of the sound and the naked, youthful energy: Hooky intent on his bass playing, Bernie diffidently concentrating on the guitar, the new boy, Stephen Morris, holding it down with minimal flourishes on the drums, but providing the meaty thwack of the snare. It struck a chord with him.

But the first time that Martin had seen Joy Division with their wunderkind lead singer perform was in the glamorous surroundings of Salford Technical College when the bill included Slaughter and the Dogs and the very glammed-up V2, whose drummer – Steve Brotherdale – had been an early drummer for JD. Martin might have been there to watch Slaughter perform, either in his capacity as band booker or to write an article for *Hot Flash* – Music Force's very own in-house magazine – or indeed because he had already recorded their single.

Whatever his reasons for being there, Martin was the one to pay the bands at the end of the night. He was attending gigs frequently at this time, usually with Suzanne at his side and a Marlboro in his mouth, sometimes shades obscuring his stoned eyes. They were an enigmatic pair. Martin was, consciously or not, on the lookout for interesting acts that he could work with and mould.

Meanwhile Rafters had become the prime venue for local, and visiting, new wave attractions. Almost every new band appeared there over a comparatively short period of time, including the Attractions themselves with leader Elvis Costello, Wayne County (who returned a year later sporting a new identity as Jayne County and the Electric Chairs), Tom Robinson, Mink Deville. There was a wonderful North-East night with Penetration and The Big G (which would eventually lead to Martin working with Pauline Murray of Penetration on her solo album), Wire, XTC and repeated performances from the locals – The Passage, Magazine, Buzzcocks, The Drones and Joy Division themselves. It became a favoured haunt for Tony Wilson, in his capacity as *So It Goes* presenter/producer. He would be there with Lindsay and it was there that his uneasy friendship and business partnership with Rob Gretton began. Gretton was one of the Rafters deejays, and edited a fanzine called *Manchester Rains*. He would become Joy Division's stalwart manager and minder and similarly look after the New Order lads right up until his untimely death on 15 May 1999.

It was Rob Gretton who actually introduced Martin to Joy Division, in late 1978. The band had already released a seven-inch independently produced extended player called *An Ideal for Living*. It had a controversial sleeve that featured a member of the Hitler Youth drumming, but it had done little business and more importantly hadn't provoked the excitement or interest that the band had hoped for. Rob's first idea was that they should record for Rabid, but Tosh Ryan was a principled socialist, and wasn't impressed with what he saw as their dodgy fascistic iconography. To this day he remains cynical about their musicianship and abilities, although the EP was distributed by the label.

It was also around this time that Ian Curtis had his first meaningful encounter with Tony Wilson. After one of the band's sets at Rafters, Ian drunkenly berated Tony for not having Joy Division on his television programme: a conversation that led to Joy Division's television debut on *Granada Reports* on 20 September 1978. *Granada Reports* was, to some, alarmingly adventurous in those days. Wilson was initially sent out to do 'semi-comic reports from the more idiosyncratic corners of the North-West' according to Mick Middles, and Tony Wilson later himself praised it as 'having been regarded as the most innovative if not hard hitting new magazine programme in the country'.

Joy Division performed just the one song – 'Shadowplay' – Ian atypically sported a pink shirt, whilst the rest of the band looked surly and uncertain in the background. Ian seemed to know instinctively how to engage with the camera, or rather let the camera find and follow him. He always knew where the camera was. He was naturally photogenic, as Anton Corbijn's pictures of the time show. The rest of the band were never as comfortable in front of the lens and later as New Order shunned publicity quite consciously. The debut performance was accompanied by some grainy, negative footage of Hulme, to suggest forward motion and travel. Ian performed his twitching, mechanistic dance that would later become so mesmerising and dangerous and copied and studied.

So when Tony Wilson, Alan Erasmus and designer Peter Saville had formed their shiny new record label and decided to record an EP, the pieces were in place for Martin Hannett and Ian Curtis to end up in a recording studio together for the first time. The studio was Cargo Studios in Rochdale, a satellite mill town of Manchester, to the north, nestling in amongst the dark satanic hills. It was owned by John Brierley and was well kitted out for the time with a number of new toys and gadgets at Martin's disposal. It was 11 October 1978.

This was the start of a fruitful relationship between band and producer, but more significantly between shaman singer and sonic magician. Joy Division entered the studio with several songs already honed down through live performance. Ian was in a state of nervous excitement. This was what he wanted to do. Martin, too, must have sensed that it was the beginning of a new chapter in his career and his aspirations. He had already recognised the potency and potential in the group and especially their oddly charismatic front man with his notebooks full of lyrics and ideas. Debbie Curtis described it as one of the most exciting and creative times for Ian. He had found his niche and his mentor. Martin knew how to honour the voice in his productions. He liked to add the vocals last, once the framework and nuts and bolts of the track had been constructed, like a stage. Then he could place the vocalist wherever he felt best for any particular song – centre stage, in the wings, off centre, in the gods, moving around restlessly. He could treat the voice with whatever was appropriate for the number – a hint of delay, a touch of echo, a slight distortion. But most of all he was able to provide Ian with the space and security to express himself and his inner soul and raw emotions, through his words and melodies and that extraordinary, mournful, prematurely mature voice, the voice that Bono would later refer to as 'the holy voice of Ian Curtis'. It is this quality of the 'performance' that is one of the key reasons why Joy Division's work has remained so enduring and affecting to successive generations. This is no pretence or artifice. This is the real deal. This comes from a dark and lonely place. Ian, led and protected by Martin, goes where angels fear to tread – to the centre of the city and the night.

The two JD tracks on *A Factory Sample* had been 'Digital' and 'Glass', the first famously named after the new AMS digital delay unit that Martin had only recently laid his hands on. 'It was digital, it was heaven sent,' Martin remarked to Jon Savage at the time. He had also begun to employ other 'tricks' including compression, reverb, repeat echoes, deliberate overload and the Marshall time modulator, which sounds as though it was one of Doctor Who's secret weapons. His aim was to create space, strangeness and 'sonic holograms'. This is when, in professional and creative terms, Martin began to ascend to some kind of zenith. It was short-lived, only really a couple of years, and these few tracks, recorded in fairly rudimentary surroundings, with pretty basic equipment, capture that surge of creative energy and plethora of ideas. He was having fun. He was enjoying the gig and sharing his enthusiasm with those around him and inspiring a clutch of new kids on the block to listen or to pick up instruments and play.

The digital delay made the instruments, especially the drums, sound crisp and clean – again the reference back to the divine disco textures and the Teutonic motorik cadences and the sounds that Bowie and Eno were exploring in their Berlin-based trilogy of albums. Martin also provided the slightly delayed echo effect on Ian's vocals that created that subtle sense of closeness between singer and listener. The songs could be heard as confessionals – linking back to their common boyhood faiths. In the recording studio, especially if the vocals are recorded separately and last, then often it can be just the vocalist and the producer and maybe an engineer who are present at the sacred, intimate moment, often in the middle of some starless and bible-black night. In effect the singer is initially communicating to, and through, his producer, his creative director, who can suggest or cajole or encourage more truth and depth, or recommend another take, or propose a different phrasing or stress. The producer can clean the vocal track so that it sounds pristine or rough, melodic or atonal, close or distant: whatever is appropriate. The producer is the first person to hear the voice and the feelings expressed through it, to understand the trajectory of the singer within the song. It is potentially a vulnerable position for a human to be in, exposed and unguarded. There is little more mystical or emotional than the sound of the bare human voice.

And Ian threw himself into the recordings of the two songs. You can hear it especially in his performance of 'Digital'. You can hear the desperation, the frustration, the elation. The barely controlled hysteria at the end of the track when Ian cries for help is a primal plea for succour and security. Martin's production gives Ian free rein and plenty of space for the patient like a good therapist would.

But if this was the start of a meaningful relationship between Ian and Martin it wasn't necessarily so for the other members of Joy Division – the back-room boys. Peter Hook, who was the most obviously forceful band member, resisted what he saw as Martin's interference. In 1997, in Mick Middles and Lindsay Reade's book *Torn Apart*, Martin is described in not altogether glowing terms: 'Bernard and I were very down to earth and he was like from another planet. He was just this really weird hippy who never talked any sense at all.'

Bernard Sumner told a *Sounds* reporter that 'Martin was into wild experimentation. He was the hippy on smack, there's no other way of putting it. And we were a band on speed. It was always that way with Martin.' It was the uneasy meeting of the speed jive Bowie boys and the smacked-out prog rocker. Martin was known to refer to them as retards, and worse besides. He once described them as 'a genius singer and three Manchester United fans', but that was more his caustic wit than any real viciousness. He would demand that they be ejected from the studio so that he could get on with making a record. One senses that the demand didn't include Ian. Martin remarked to the journalist Jon Savage that 'There used to be a lot of room in their [Joy Division's] music and they were a gift to a producer, 'cos they didn't have a clue, they didn't argue.'

Chris Hewitt, another alternative local character and promoter and entrepreneur and fundamentally well-meaning old hippy, was, and is, a great admirer of Martin's work. When I interviewed him in 2006 he reckoned that 'Martin Hannett was the secret of Joy Division. Ian had some great ideas for lyrics and an interesting voice but at the time the band was no great shakes. Martin added all sorts of interesting sounds and textures and turned them into something special. No one really appreciated how much he did. He took ordinary bands and turned them into something else.'

Chris also knew that Martin could be generous with his time and skills, unmotivated by greed. He feels that Martin was underrated as a musician and unfairly portrayed as a drug-addled lunatic. Mick Middles thinks that Martin had a profound effect on Joy Division's sound: 'Hannett was the link really that changed everything.'

There are others who feel that Joy Division themselves had progressed and sharpened up through constant rehearsing (in TJ Davidson's freezing cold, gloomy rehearsal studios) and frequent gigging and that Hannett's influence has been overrated.

It was most likely the combination of various factors, but inevitably a live number changes in the studio and the sound, feel and production of the recorded song is maintained in further live explorations. You can hear evidence of that on the live sides of *Still*.

After the unexpected success and acclaim that greeted *A Factory Sample*, and chiefly Joy Division's contributions to it, the now more confident, even cocky, Factory Records team decided it was time to venture into a higher class of studio and record an entire album with Joy Division. It was the right band in the right place at the right time with the right Man. The band was Joy Division, the place was Strawberry Studios, Stockport, the time was April 1979 and the Man was Martin Hannett.

Strawberry Studios was altogether a different proposition from Cargo. This was a state-of-the-art recording boutique with all the flash gear and creature comforts that you might expect. It had a shiny new look, with shiny new equipment and a legendary air conditioning system. It housed 24-track recording equipment – a gleaming mixing desk that Martin would almost caress. It was plush and comfortable and discreet. It always had a hushed atmosphere about it and once inside one instinctively lowered one's voice. It was demure, rather than flashy. It was quiet, rather than loud. It had good vibrations. It had a downstairs pool table where the lads could hang out and act out their machismo and demonstrate their backstreet credentials. There was a coffee machine, considered something of a luxury in those days. There was even a reception area and usually a glamorous receptionist on duty. It was deluxe and delightful. It had been built by the highly successful Kennedy Street Enterprises and had been home most memorably to 10cc and their massive recording of their number one international hit 'I'm Not in Love', which at the time, and perhaps even since, employed more vocal overdubs than any other recording. Tony Wilson liked to tell tales of Martin's supposed erratic behaviour there. In one story, Martin jumped up from the producer's chair and shouted: 'What's that? What's that gold shiny thing? It's not a halo. I'm not dead. Am I dead?' To which Ian Curtis purportedly replied: 'No Martin, it's a gold disc. 10cc, "I'm Not in Love".'

'I'm not in 10cc am I?' said Martin.

Ian reassured him: 'No Martin, you're not in 10cc. You're in Stockport.'

Whether this is true, or just another Martin Hannett legend, Strawberry Studios became a second home for Martin for the next few years. Even if he didn't record there he liked to take the master tapes there to mix. The pub across the road was The Waterloo and there is a common misconception that Martin spent more of his time drinking in that hostelry than he did working in the studio. By this time Martin was using significant amounts of heroin. Heroin and alcohol just don't mix; in fact alcohol can dull the effects of narcotics and even increase the attendant nausea. Martin was scientific in his drug usage and knew the properties of the substances and the contraindications. But more importantly he was motivated by the task in hand and especially by the prospect of working with Ian over a longer time span and a varied collection of songs. Martin's, and Ian's, moment had arrived.

Even though Debbie Curtis was in the final term of her pregnancy she noticed how upbeat and positive and genuinely inspired her husband seemed. He was, however, pulled between the worlds of artistic creation and the fruits of human creation. It was perhaps another tension that contributed to the otherworldly and yet intensely personal nature of the album.

Lindsay Reade later commented that the band gave 'the impression that they were really enjoying themselves, that they were completely happy in that environment . . . for the most part they seemed content to let Martin take control'. And of course control was immensely important to Ian. He had matured swiftly and had assumed the mantle of leader of the gang, probably with Hooky as his right-hand man; the brawn behind the brains. But Ian knew the soundscape and atmosphere that he wanted, that he could hear in his head and see in his dreams and he knew that Martin Hannett was perhaps the only person who could create it.

Martin therefore created a sound and an ambience that was far removed from JD's live noise. It seems to exist in its own world, with only distant echoes of the real world. It is punky and psychedelic. It is speed and smack. It is cerebral and visceral.

The album is dominated by the voice and personality and hopes and fears of the central protagonist – Ian Curtis – under the direction, supervision and tutelage of Martin Hannett. Paul Morley commented that '[Martin] did an extraordinary job and all great albums in history, whether it's the Beatles or U2, Bowie, Pink Floyd, they all have a great producer who is making it happen.' The other members of the band noticed that Martin seemed to have a special relationship with Ian. He made Ian as at ease as possible when in the studio; or chatting to him in The Waterloo, 'it was apparent that Martin was building some kind of intimacy there,' according to Peter Hook. It could even have been a cynical ploy on Martin's part in order to obtain the best possible performances from Ian, because Martin knew that *his* future career and reputation would rest heavily on the reaction to this recording.

Mick Middles feels that Ian had really found his voice, lyrically and emotionally, during the *UP* sessions and had also willingly accepted the mantle of leader. During the sessions he was happy to make suggestions, to suggest embellishments or arrangements and to negotiate with Martin about the structure and textures of the tracks. Lindsay Reade noticed that 'There was a special closeness between Martin and Ian . . . it was kind of private between themselves'. It was born out of mutual respect and a curious dependency. Ian depended on Martin to realise the scale of his dreams and visions and Martin perhaps needed Ian to express and exorcise some of his own demons. And their fates were inextricably linked from this point onwards, creatively, publicly and indeed financially. Martin will always be remembered as the guy who produced *Unknown Pleasures*. It is another reason why Martin was so devastated by Ian's sudden suicidal death. A part of Martin's psyche died when Ian killed himself. He lost his lightning conductor; he lost his voice; he lost his way; he lost his meal ticket.

But although Martin and Ian worked closely and intensely in the studio together, they seldom, if ever, spent time together socially. Martin was not one to 'hang out with the band', especially a group that was suspicious of his methods and his character. Stephen Morris gave an insight into working with Martin:

'One time I was moonlighting by playing drums on a John Cooper Clarke album that Martin was producing at the same time as *Unknown Pleasures*. I did about three takes of one track and there was silence from the control room. Eventually he said, 'Yeah it's OK – do it again but this time make it a bit more . . . cocktail party.'

His seemingly eccentric methods included the oft-told story about dismantling Stephen Morris's drum kit and also getting Steve to play his drum kit on the roof.

'Martin wanted everything recorded separately, so we started with just the bass drum – literally the bass drum and me. Then the snare again and then the hi-hat again,' Morris explained in an article in 2005, before adding graciously: 'I can understand what he wanted, with the benefit of hindsight, but at the time I couldn't see the point of it.'

There is also the story of Martin suggesting to Bernie, in his role as guitarist, that he play the song faster, but slower. Other tales would have you believe that Martin also wanted harder, but softer and louder, but quieter.

Famously Jon Savage once asked Martin about the sound of the lift in the opening of 'Insight', and was told by Martin, 'That's a lift.' It was indeed the creaky old freight lift in Strawberry that was used for transporting equipment up and down. The image and sound of The Lift feature in the album and also in John Cooper Clarke's lyrics. Martin liked to be in motion, in a lift, or a car or a plane. When one is travelling, even briefly in an elevator, for that time you are removed from the daily struggle, you are in a no man's land; you're neither here nor there. It is also the sense of forward motion and purpose, of propulsion, that Martin captures in most of his productions.

Similarly, sounds of glass and references to glass litter Joy Division's output. Breaking glass is such an obvious, yet potent, image and often conjures up scenes of domestic, as well as military, violence. The hand smashing through the glass panel; the pint glass smashed in drunken anger; the body hurtling through the windscreen. It features loudly and vividly on the final track of *UP*, 'I Remember Nothing'. Martin uses prolonged delay on the guitar and swashes of sinister synth that swirl like mist around Ian's fractured vocalising. As in Martin's work with JCC it is clear that he understood and honoured the emotional landscape of the song and the meaning, and subtext, of the lyrics. Again this is what gives the album such depth, such clarity and such resonance and what makes it so enduring.

On a more technical note it is Martin's judicious use of the digital delay that gives the album its unique feel and presence. Martin chose a minute report time so the delay is almost imperceptible. You can feel, rather than hear, the effect. Vini Reilly, who has made auspicious use of effects and delay units on his guitars throughout his illustrious career, including his beloved WEM Copycat, explained Martin's technique:

'Martin used that digital delay not as a repeat echo delay but to make a tiny millisecond that came so close to the drum it was impossible to hear. I would never have thought of doing that. Nobody would. I don't know how he could have possibly envisaged the final sound.'

The resultant *Unknown Pleasures* album itself, recorded in a matter of weeks, saw a quantum leap for JD, from the sometimes brash thrash of their live output to something altogether weightier, more steeped in significance, and indeed more melodic. The spare, but crucial, addition of synthesiser lines underlined and highlighted the tunes.

It *is* a melodic record. The aspect of *Unknown Pleasures* that is sometimes overlooked is its danceability on certain tracks, no more so than on the near-disco-rock of 'She's Lost Control'. Live, Ian's dancing to that number was always a highlight as his rhythmic, spasmodic movements became more frantic. The tragedy obviously was that his epilepsy was taking hold and was agitated by the stroboscopic lights and indeed the jerky rhythms themselves. Famously, in later gigs, Ian would 'lose control' and spin across the stage and collide with the equipment and collapse into Steve Morris's drum kit and the crowd would cheer, imagining that it was all part of some post-James Brown, postmodern punk funk, stage routine. After the gigs Ian could be seen shivering and shaking, sometimes, like the Godfather of Soul himself, wrapped in a blanket.

Similarly 'Disorder' has that discoid feel seamlessly sewn into the arrangement and production. This was a post-punk strand, the meeting of punk rock and European, Giorgio Moroder/Conny Plank-styled disco that would be picked up by Simple Minds, Ultravox, Japan, Siouxsie and the Banshees, The Cure and even be woven into the cloth of goth, especially Danse Society, March Violets and the later Sisters of Mercy albums – *Floodland* and *Vision Thing*.

Likewise Ian's baritone croon and bass mumblings, languid phrasing and emotive pitching, would have an influence on other singers of the period, particularly the proto-goths such as Pete Murphy from Bauhaus, Andrew Eldritch (perhaps the best exponent of the ghostly bass croon, the basso profondo) from Sisters of Mercy and his great rival Wayne Hussey of The Mission. In an interview I did with Jon Savage in 2007, he told me that Andrew Eldritch had been desperate to work with Martin Hannett and had been hugely influenced by him. Indeed I remember seeing all of Sisters of Mercy's recorded output – the Merciful Release EPs and singles in their eye-catching dark green and blood red sleeves – on Martin's 'desk' in his flat in Didsbury.

The fingerprints of *Unknown Pleasures* are all over subsequent bands and albums and even today can be heard clearly in the recordings of Interpol, Radio 4, Snow Patrol, Doves, Elbow and Radiohead. The album had an enormous effect on U2, which Bono has often acknowledged, from the way they structure the dynamics of their songs to the manner in which they use The Edge's guitar to add texture, tone and colour. It can also be heard in the recordings of Southern Death Cult and their vocalist Ian Astbury's phrasing in later Cult albums. It has been argued that although *Unknown Pleasures* has been cited as a 'goth' album it far transcends that genre. What makes it essentially different from the goth canon is its authenticity. In other words some goth bands are accused of theatricality, artifice and an over-preoccupation with horror, graves, skulls, Bela Lugosi, the Undead, darkness and terror, which can slip into pantomime and Grand Guignol if left unchecked. Although Ian Curtis's lyrics do use images of death and darkest chambers, they almost always retain a personal and indeed domestic angle that saves them from forced theatricality.

Ian loved the final result. He, and Martin, had created a masterpiece that could be rated up there amongst the albums and artists that Ian so admired – The Velvet Underground's debut, David Bowie's *Low*, Iggy Pop's *The Idiot*, Roxy Music's *For Your Pleasure*. Now Joy Division were potentially a major-league proposition, who would be seen as key contenders in the New Rock marketplace, with a groundbreaking album under their long grey coats. It was a work of art.

The other members of Joy Division, however, were not happy with the results. Years later, in the sleeve notes for the boxed set *Heart and Soul*, Bernie Sumner stated:

'We resented it, but Rob [Gretton] loved it, Wilson loved it, and the press loved it, and the public loved it . . . we swallowed our pride and went with it.'

Now, years after Ian's death, it is written about in reverential terms, as a sacrament, an article of faith. The black (none blacker) and grey cover, with the now iconic Peter Saville imagery, the minimalist lettering, the merest information, all add to the mystery and mystique. It is seen as a landmark album. Perhaps one of the recordings that encapsulate the notion of post-punk.

Whatever it was, it would change Ian Curtis's and Martin Hannett's lives and careers immeasurably.

Back in 1979, in the dragon's den of the magician himself, I hear it for the very first time.

'So . . . what do you think?'

There is genuine vulnerability in Martin's voice.

'Martin, it's a fucking miracle.'

9

Who Killed Martin Hannett?

It is an early spring day in 1979.

Paul Humphreys and Andy McCluskey, who collectively are Orchestral Manoeuvres in the Dark, have got a bounce in their step and their young lives and early dreams ahead of them. They are going into the already legendary Strawberry Studios, Stockport with the already legendary Martin 'Zero' Hannett to record their (now legendary) first single 'Electricity', which will be backed by the (now 'almost' forgotten) 'Almost'. Previously they have rehearsed and recorded some demos in the garage of their then manager's house on an old four-track Teac.

Martin dispenses with introductions, which further intimidates the two young hopefuls. The band has been sent to him, in his role of Factory Records in-house producer. They have been signed to Factory Records because Tony Wilson's (then) wife, the lovely Lindsay, thinks it would be a good idea and the fact that they are handsome, charming young Liverpudlians with an ear for a catchy melody and a futurist setting has not escaped her attention.

Their equipment (two keyboards) has been set up by a lackey, but Martin spends another hour messing around with a 32-band equaliser and other giant FX, before he even considers listening to their post-modern, Kraftwerk-influenced post-industrial pop songs.

They eventually take up positions and are overawed by the quality and sheer volume of the foldback. They play through 'Electricity' with its gorgeous melodic structure, faux-naive lyrics, tinkling, chiming rhythm and infectious hooks. Their temporary manager, who got the job because he has a van, comes through to the 'live' room.

'He's asleep.'

'What?' Andy can barely hear, so deafening has been the sound.

'He crawled under the mixing desk while you were playing and fell asleep; well it was more like he just lost consciousness.'

'Is he ill?' Paul wonders in a concerned tone.

'The assistant engineer lad didn't seem to even notice,' the manager adds.

They go back into the control room. Sure enough Martin Zero, the post-punk hero, is curled up in a foetal position under the impressive console, fast asleep.

'Maybe he's narcoleptic,' Paul suggests thoughtfully.

'Maybe he's just narco,' Andy replies rather more realistically, with Scouse quick wit.

'You wake him up then,' Paul suggests.

'No, you wake him up,' Andy answers.

They bat it back and forth for a while.

The assistant lad makes them all a cup of tea.

Martin doesn't budge an inch.

'I hope he's not dead,' Paul says.

'Not yet,' Martin grumbles as he uncurls, stands up and shakes his tangled curls.

Paul looks at Andy. Andy looks at Paul. Andy shrugs.

'I got that one, very pretty. Now play me the other one,' Martin suggests forcefully.

Andy looks at Paul. Paul shrugs.

They return to their keyboards. After all this is post-punk.

In the event they chose not to use the recordings of the tracks that they did with Martin. Andy felt that Hannett's take on 'Electricity' was 'too lush' and they went for a more poppy, brighter sound, which pragmatically and commercially was probably the right decision. But in a recent interview that I did with Andy he was still full of praise for the 'spiritual' quality that Martin brought to his production of 'Almost', turning it into an ethereal, hymnlike lament.

10

I had no idea, when I first saw Stephanie Formula, that she was staying with Martin in the hopped-up hepcat Hannett hotel. I also had no idea that her boyfriend was the synth player in the mighty Magazine – the Kafkaesque combo that Howard Devoto put together after leaving the Buzzcocks. But Stephanie and Dave were not married at the time – she was only called Stephanie Formula for convenience – and they had decided to have a break from their liaison. It was entirely common in those days – relationships were much more open and fluid. The night I met her Dave Formula was down in London working on the final Magazine album. (This was the Martin-produced, funk punk meisterwerk that would become *The Correct Use of Soap*.)

It is early 1979.

Another night in the Factory, Russell Club, that goes on for ever, fuelled by amphetamine sulphate par excellence, amyl nitrate, Black Julie's beef-free burgers, piss poor lager, endless enthusiasm, creative explosions, chance meetings, random rendezvous, Xeroxed fanzines, ripped jeans, torn apart hearts, Buzzcocks badges asking 'What do I get?' or proclaiming 'Shit!' or more obscure arty *Pink Flag* badges (the first Wire album, darlings of the conceptualists), crazy-colour pliers-cut spiky peroxide hair, retro Cramps-influenced bouffants, strawberry-flavoured hairspray, gooey green gel, tepid tap water, unfocused anarcho-politico leanings, Trotsky rockers, strange imaginings, forbidden fruit, primal pogoing and an undertow of menace and latent aggression.

Peter Saville is there that night with his divine decadent debutante Snow White Julie sporting a pink vinyl 45 on her lacquered do. The place is the Russell Club. The band list could include darlings of the intelligentsia The Passage, a nascent nubile Certain Ratio, Pete Shelley's pet project and boyfriends The Tiller Boys, Linder in her band off-the-wall Ludus, Cabaret Voltaire in their strictly uncommercial phase, John Dowie doing his punky stand-up act, John the Postman as ever freeforming his endless version of 'Louie Louie'. It could also include the Distractions, the Lurkers, Swell Maps, Teardrop Explodes, the anodyne Echo and the Bunnymen, the adenoidal Addix, Spizz Energi, Spizz Oil, Athletico Spizz and Gordon the Moron as compère.

It's between sets that I approach Stephanie. The Buzzcocks' 'Ever Fallen in Love (with Someone You Shouldn't've)' is playing. Soon afterwards, she takes me back, in a Manc black cab, to the Hannett hotel.

'You never told me you live in Martin and Suzanne's flat.'

'You never asked.'

Martin and Suzanne are snuggled up together on the sofa. Suzanne is wearing her trademark blue leather jacket – like Martin she is always chilly, though seldom chilled in the new-millennium sense. Her long, willowy legs are tucked up under her perfect bum.

Martin is watching himself on *The Old Grey Whistle Test*, possibly on a video recording. Martin was one of the first people to get a brand new video recorder. On screen the camera pans lazily past him as he sits playing his bass guitar, curly hair falling in his face, concentrating on the notes. He is in his role as part of the uber-rhythm section of The Invisible Girls. Steve Hopkins is suave, with handsome matinée idol good looks and looks like an escapee from the Ritz Ballroom as he tinkles the ivories. Is that John Scott from Absurd Records on guitar? Could it be Paul Burgess from the already sadly passé Sad Café on drums? No one is entirely sure now.

Suzanne gives me a rather haughty look. She does haughty with aplomb.

'Hello Col. Hello Stephanie. I see you two have met.'

'We're watching The Invisible Girls. Although from this vantage point, this point of view, they look very visible, to me. Far too visible,' says Martin.

'Magazine have stayed down in London. They're doing a few gigs. I think they're playing the Moonlight Club tonight.' Suzanne snipes in a scarcely veiled attempt to make us feel guilty. Once a Catholic, always a Catholic: you can take the girl out of the holy mass, but you can't take the holy mass out of the girl.

'Aye, they're gigging in t'Smoke,' Martin jokes, trying to lighten the mood. 'Christ I look fat!' he announces with real disgust as the camera lingers on him for a moment before returning to the rake-thin angular shape that is Johnny Clarke.

'We don't want to keep you two up past your bedtime,' Suzanne sneers with obvious disdain.

'Do I really look that fat? Be honest. Be brutally frigging honest. Am I porky? And don't tell any porky pies!' Martin makes fun of himself but underneath there is real concern. There is always the fatty within, the inner lardy, waiting to get out. Suzanne runs her long fingers affectionately through Martin's tangled mane. He relaxes a little, but still shakes his head in disbelief at the televisual representation of himself.

And so it is that I spend a great deal of the next fortnight at Martin's parvenu apartment. I get to see the domestic Martin. Martin in his jim-jams; Martin eating Frosties for brekkie like Daddy Bear; Martin and Suzanne cooking a passable Irish stew (Martin's diet of apples, cheese and speed had faltered. From now on he was prone to put on the pounds, sometimes at an astonishing rate, almost as though he was swelling up. Even his head would look fatter and his face could take on a bloated, debauched look); Martin asking Suzanne if they have a Hoover; Martin reading the inky music papers – *NME*, *Melody Maker*, *Sounds* – and alternating between feigned indifference and frigging indignation at their sloppy comments or overblown critiques of his, and his contemporaries', recorded output. ('*Unknown Pleasures* may very well be one of the best, white, English, debut LPs of the year' – Jon Savage, *Melody Maker*, 21 July 1979.)

I meet a trickle of passing sub-celebrities including John Cooper Clarke, Ed Banger, Gordon the Moron, Linder from Ludus, Eric Random, Jilted John and indeed Jon Savage. Martin and I meet in the kitchen and have ridiculously sweet cups of Typhoo tea: we both take four sugars. We dunk bourbons. He tries to introduce me to the dangerous delights of Jammie Dodgers, but it's a bridge too far.

We play the 'what's your favourite . . . album' game.

The *White Album* with its eclectic range of songs and experimentation is surprisingly his choice for fave Fab Four elpee, whereas I go for perhaps the more obvious choice of *Revolver*. We discover that we share a sneaky preference for *Their Satanic Majesties Request* by the Rolling Stones over their other prolific recorded output. This will be borne out, many years from now, in 1990, by Martin's homage in Tony Ogden's World of Twist to 'She's a Rainbow', which, whilst remaining true and faithful to the detail and delicacy of the original, adds a further contemporary and dancey edge: psychedelia for the E generation. Of course we are both fans of Brian Jones (*Who Killed Christopher Robin?*) and Syd Barrett (*Lost in the Woods*). I go for *Blonde on Blonde*, he opts for *Highway 61 Revisited*, in the Dylan section. We even confess a secretive affection for Sunshine Superman Hurdy Gurdy Donovan and Iron Butterfly's opus 'In-A-Gadda-Da-Vida'.

Our Top Ten Movies Ever diversion reveals that Antonioni's *Blowup* is one of our mutual favourite films. We devise a system of points and then calculate a combined list – I have no idea now how it worked, but we are both mighty pleased with it. It also includes *The Graduate*, *Dr Strangelove*, *One Flew Over the Cuckoo's Nest* – which at that instant was fairly recent – *Lolita*, *What Ever Happened to Baby Jane?*, *Cape Fear*, *In the Heat of the Night*, *Rebel without a Cause* and, a surprising choice here, *West Side Story*, probably due to Leonard Bernstein's incomparable soundtrack and the fluid, quintessentially cool jazz dance. Martin like any good magpie artist takes his influences from here, there and everywhere. You gotta be eclectic if you're going to be electric. But it's probably fair to say that this obsession with bests and lists is the mild end of the autistic continuum.

One weekend, Steph told me that Dave Formula (né Tomlinson, a much less electronic, glamorous name) was coming up for the weekend and they were going to attempt some sort of reconciliation, so I made myself scarce and spent some time in the tiny upstairs flat on Mauldeth Road that I was renting. I enjoyed a long, sleepless weekend of mandatory sex, dirty drugs and post-rock and roll. I even found time to go and see Joy Division play an impressive and prestigious gig at Manchester's Lesser Free Trade Hall.

The Joy Boys are supported by an unaccompanied John Cooper Clarke who is in fine form and looks as though he might have eaten a bag of chips some time in the last month. He rattles (did he ever do it another way?) through some oldies but goldies including 'Twat', 'You Never See a Nipple in the Daily Express', 'Kung Fu International' and 'Majorca' as well as motor-mouthing some more recent rhymes like 'Conditional Discharge' and 'Evidently Chickentown', which for my money suffers from the lack of the wired-up drum machine and scattergun instrumentation that Martin wrapped it in on the Rabid Records recorded version.

It proves to be a bit of a self-congratulatory night for the right night people. I suspect that everyone is on the guest list or at least anyone who is anyone. It's the post-punk, new glam glitterati. Present are members of The Members, Buzzcocks, The Fall, Crispy Ambulance and Biting Tongues. Long raincoats are beginning to put in an appearance, as are The Raincoats themselves. There's a busload of Scousers come over from Liverpool, representing the new wave of smoother synthesiser combos like Orchestral Manoeuvres in the Dark, Dalek I Love You and the rockier The Mighty Wah!.

Joy Division themselves are magnificent. They suddenly seem like a proper band with an impressive sound system and roadies and technicians and all the paraphernalia of imminent success. Ian does his mesmeric epileptic dance, his youthful voice booms and speaks of inner demons, turmoil and yearns for release and redemption. Hooky keeps his head down and his six-string bass slung low. Steve Morris, perhaps under Martin's fierce tutelage, has become an accomplished and creative drummer. He has incorporated syndrums, the Simmonds twin-channel synthesiser, the Musicaid Claptrap, the Boss DR55 drum machine and electronic plates into his Rogers concert kit. These are all toys and gadgets that he has acquired as a result of working with Martin. Bernie keeps out of the light, providing washes and runs on his Shergold Custom Masquerader. Bernie flashily swaps guitars mid-set, exchanging the Shergold for a Gibson. Ian even straps on his Vox Phantom 4 Special, with its coffinlike shape, more for effect and image, perhaps, than added musicality.

Their extended set includes favourites like 'Transmission' when everyone joins in throatily on the 'dance, dance, dance to the radio' chorus ('dance' pronounced in the Northern style), 'She's Lost Control', heavily featuring Steve's armoury of syn-FX, a revisited, revitalised, dancey 'Digital', a sombre slowed-down 'Shadowplay', a discordant 'Disorder', before introducing more solemn and stately material like 'Decades' and 'Passover', that will feature on the *Closer* album.

They seem remote and distant on the unfriendly stage. They have lost some of the urgency and immediacy of their live shows at Band on the Wall or Rafters or even, going back to their Warsaw roots, at The Electric Circus. I imagine tours of Europe, Japan, Australasia and

America in concert halls and eventually stadia. They encore with a new song. It is called 'Love Will Tear Us Apart'.

Martin is not at the gig. Tony Wilson is there bustling around importantly, whilst wife Lindsay looks demure and aloof. There are journalists from the inky music press of the Nick Kent, Charles Shaar Murray and Tony Parsons school of new journalism – who's afraid of Tom Wolfe? Jon Savage is present representing the Manchester journalism contingent, as is an anxious Paul Morley. Rifts have come to be revealed between the main Factory players. Martin is already harbouring delusions that he is somehow being cheated out of profits. He has also been stung by the negative reaction and comments from some of Joy Division about his production work on *Unknown Pleasures* – he will rarely see them play live after this, arguing that the live versions of their songs lose the subtlety and depth of the recorded versions. He is communicating less and less with his partners and is starting to experience himself as the maverick genius, the oddball outsider. Tony is enjoying his role as Record Label Mogul and Multi-Media Man: he is on the lookout for new groups to add to Factory's roster. He is managing A Certain Ratio, his new kids off their blocks. Rob Gretton has taken on the role of surly, overprotective JD manager with aplomb and Alan Erasmus is forever the quiet one, getting on with the business in the background. Peter Saville has upped and gone down to London and is in demand as designer for a number of new acts including OMD. Everyone wants a slice of the neo-classical action. Everyone wants to be like Factory Records, apart form Martin who wants something else, although he's never sure exactly what.

By this point, my brief tenure as vocalist with The Durutti Column has come to an end. I suspect that Martin and I are the only ones who enjoyed the tracks we did for *A Factory Sample*. (To this day Vini Reilly totally dissociates himself from them.) After those sessions, Vini and I had 'rehearsed' a few times at my flat in Mauldeth Road. Vini improvised fragile tunes on his Les Paul guitar, feeding the chords and notes through his WEM Copycat, whilst I extemporised fairly abstract lyrics/vocal sounds over the top. We played two very short sets at the Factory Club – one opening for Slaughter and the Dogs, when we were spat at and bottled off stage; the second time to a more appreciative audience when we supported Magazine. But there seemed little future in it. Vini's health was deteriorating and he had no appetite for live performance, so he went off to do his instrumental thing and create his first album – *The Return of the Durutti Column* – with Martin accompanying and producing, whilst I formed a 'proper' new wave glam punk outfit – The Roaring 80s. My bass player John Hurst is present but he is in deep discussion with Alan Hempsall from Crispy Ambulance organising his move into record production.

I start to feel somewhat paranoid. I have taken too much speed yet again; I haven't slept for two nights and I don't have any gear to bring me down. Martin is conspicuous by his absence. I wish he was there. There are rumours that other, less brilliant, producers are interested in working with Joy Division – Colin Thurston, Mike Thorne, Martin Rushent are mentioned. These are young Turks; pretenders to the throne. Even the holy name of Eno is being whispered reverently amongst the cognoscenti and the post-punk Politburo. Everything is new, fresh and shiny, reflecting Peter Saville's clean, neo-classical designs. I feel grubby and passé. I am in my glam punk phase. I am wearing my (hopefully) trademark red trousers, lurid pink blousy shirt and regulation Lewis Leathers punk-rocker zippy jacket. But I notice a distinct lack of leather. I feel like The Clash's '(White Man) in Hammersmith Palais'. I seem to be the only one wearing any colours. Everyone else is in studied shades of grey, black or dark blue. They fade to grey. There is actual evidence of trench coats.

I am in the foyer of the Lesser Free. People are starting to drift off; I have heard talk of an after-gig party that I've not been invited to, adding to my uneasy, queasy sense of mounting paranoia and persecution. I don't know if Martin has been invited either: is he already becoming persona non grata? Are we being excluded because of our mutual propensity for 'hard drugs'? No one wants a junkie hanging around, not even other junkies eventually. It happens very quickly. Around this period CP Lee, who has been best mates with Martin dating back to 1969, has banned him from his flat, in hope of a tough love intervention.

I think that I'm going to vomit, but I haven't eaten anything for so long that my stomach lining is digesting itself in a brave attempt to provide me with some sustenance. John Hurst and the drummer from Crispy Ambulance call over –

'Are you going to the party? It's in Northenden somewhere.'

I call back – 'Maybe baby,' in a feeble attempt to be cool and hip and insouciant.

I make it to a toilet, into a cubicle and collapse onto my knees in supplication to the ceramic bowl with the legend SHANKS in blue lettering. I dry retch. Nothing comes up but bile and disappointment.

I hear two male fans come into the bogs and unbutton their fashionably baggy grey trousers to have a slash.

'They're brilliant live,' says Fan 1.

'It's a shame that Michael Hamlet guy ruined them in the studio,' opines Fan 2.

'Well what do you expect? He's a prog rocker,' Fan 1 states haughtily. There could have been no greater insult at the time than to accuse someone of being a 'prog rocker'.

I feel indignant and incensed on Martin's behalf, but too weak to even get to my feet. I heave again. My throat burns; my eyes water.

'He's on his way out for sure,' Fan 2 suggests callously.

'Even the stuff he did with Buzzcocks is pretty shit if you ask me,' Fan 1 sneers derisively as they zip up on their tiny pricks. They are a couple of tiny pricks.

I gasp for air and sanctuary.

'And what about that crap he did with that Donny Clark geezer?' They don't even have the decency to get the name right or to wash their hands.

I push myself up onto my feet. The porcelain tiles are far too bright. I splash my face with cold water. I have a crumpled wrap of sulphate in my pocket. I retreat back into the cubicle, bolt the door, kneel again, this time the supplicant to the Greater God Speed, and snort up half of the remaining white powder.

I stagger swiftly out of the Gentlemen's lavatory.

The foyer of the Manchester Lesser Free Trade Hall is entirely deserted. Even Fan 1 and Fan 2 have disappeared. I have twenty quid in my wallet. I feel trapped and ensnared.

I spend the night in my empty house, staring at the ceiling.

Not much later, it transpired that Stephanie and Dave were going to give it another go. From then on my relationship with Stephanie was pretty much dead in the water.

This meant the end of my domestic encounters with Martin. No more chance encounters in the kitchen. No more obsessive Top Ten lists. No more sweet cups of tea. No more sweetness.

11

It was a typical night out for the two of us.

In my mind are vivid snapshots, underscored by music – a show reel of the kind of trip that we used to go on.

It is late 1979.

It begins, and ends, in Martin's uterine Volvo estate.

It starts in the late evening: dusk. Martin, picking me up from my house. This is the point of departure; this is the point of view. We are in a position of strength. We both have some gear, albeit a quarter of a gram. The worst time to go and score is when you're withdrawing – you'll take any piddly shit at any exorbitant price. We are both on the good foot. Martin is still in the ascendant – his work with Buzzcocks, Joy Division, Magazine has been noted, lauded and he is being courted and fêted by the big fish in the big pond and even some of the bigger fish over the bigger pond. There are rumours of him working with U2, Simple Minds, Ultravox, The Psychedelic Furs and The Only Ones. They always want you when you're up, but nobody wants you when you're down and out.

My glam Gestapo outfit The Roaring 80s is looking tasty, at least in my head. My thespian career is healthy. Oh yes sirree we are a couple of renaissance men; a pair of power players. I'm a shaker, he's a mover. I'm a groover, he's a maker. I am attired in après Nouvelle Vague Oxfam chic – baggy grey trousers with turn-ups, second-hand striped herringbone jacket, crumpled collarless cream dress shirt (the starchy detachable collar long discarded and forgotten), off-white tennis shoes with no trace of laces. My hair has grown out of the peroxide pink spike and is now approaching dark red floppy. Even Martin, under the auspices of Suzanne, is looking pretty neat in straight blue jeans and matching denim jacket, collar turned up against the cold, real or imagined, and he has allowed her to take some shears to his locks so that they are marginally less messy and curly. He is, as ever, unshaven. He, unexpectedly, has on a pair of red baseball boots. His weight seems to have dropped again, probably in direct correlation to the amount of speed he is using during the day: speed through the day, smack down at night.

'Oh yeah, I did this for you,' I say.

It's a cassette of lovingly compiled tracks from the Krautrock albums that I am currently enamoured with to the point of obsession and that Martin has expressed an avid interest in. There are tracks from the first two Neu! albums, confusingly both called *Neu!*, as well as the first two La Düsseldorf epic elpees. This is motorik at its finest and most propulsive. This stuff is hugely influential on Martin the Producer Artist. The productions are built around the drums, which have become the main melodic instrument. Around the insistent, cyclical rhythms, created in real time on real kits, buzz and vibrate all kinds of interesting sounds, flanged and phased guitars, pulsing bass and muted synthesisers. It is stripped down, ultramodern and minimalist. It is the sound of the autobahn and the Trans-Europe Express rather than the parochial British motorway or the meandering A roads of middle England. It evokes images of European cities such as Berlin, Bonn, Cologne, Brussels, Geneva, Zurich, Munich, Milan and Vienna. It is sleek and sophisticated, clinical and clean on the surface but with an undertow of muted emotionalism and melancholy. If you want to understand Martin's aesthetic and sensibility at this time and the influence it has brought to bear on the creation of *Unknown Pleasures* and then *Closer* and *The Correct Use of Soap*, these are the tracks to listen to. He takes the European soundscapes and transforms them into something uniquely English: the sound of the A1 and the M6; the musical lingo of the Leeds intersection. Martin's soundstage is always rooted in North-West England, always returning to his beginnings in the deserted mill towns and the echoing clang of the abandoned machinery.

Martin presses the C90 into his deluxe player. The first Neu! track – 'Hallogallo' – filters in. It provides the ideal soundtrack for the first phase of our journey. It is perfect driving music. We both nod our heads to the insistent click-clack of the rhythm track and the backwards guitars. I am pulsating away myself on a well-measured cocktail of high-grade sulphate, some top-notch cocaine leavened with a healthy helping of heroin. Martin is motoriking away on a similar concoction. This is narcotic music made by people on narcotics about the effects and experience of narcotics for listeners on narcotics. This is as close to some of the stuff that Martin is helping to create as you will get. It tries to capture those ambient, peripheral sounds and sonic sensations that the hardened narcotic addict accepts as a daily part of the internal soundtrack. That is why many of Martin's productions are so seductive and addictive. A great deal of what he does in the studio is to weave in almost subliminal texture and tones. The sound is a medicine. It stones you to your soul.

But it is not enough: there are serious drugs to be found.

Rushing through underilluminated streets on the way to the dealer's we change the soundtrack to The Clash's first album – the song is their white reggae version of Junior Murvin's 'Police and Thieves'. Martin turns the volume up to 11. It is late evening. The people of south Manchester are going about their nocturnal trade. Mothers hurrying to fish and chip emporia; petty thieves putting on woollen gloves and balaclavas; alcoholic dads breaking into piggy banks; streetwalkers starting to strut the streets; middle-aged middle-market men cruising in their Vauxhall Cavaliers and Ford Escorts looking for nubile flesh to procure.

At the dealer's – Kath's – domicile, the door is opened by Big Ken. He has just come out of prison. (He has always 'just come out of prison', apart from when he is in prison or on remand.) He smells of pubs and Wormwood Scrubs. He looks lost, even though he's in his own porch. He is very big and usually very docile. I suspect that he might have had several courses of electroconvulsive therapy.

'Kath, it is Martine's fella and . . . and that producer bloke.'

I see Martin cringe and wonder if he might have a change of heart, but the allure of splendid scag is too strong to resist.

'I'm in the kitchen. I'll put a brew on,' Kath screeches from beyond.

The sitting room is immaculate. There are now two children's push-bikes parked in the corner, but no sight of any children. On the shelves are even more youngsters' toys – Dinky cars, tiny garages, plastic soldiers, London Bobbies, Sindys, Barbies. 'How much is a gram?' Martin asks bluntly.

'A gram?' Ken repeats as though he has no idea what that could mean.

'Yes, a gram of heroin. You do sell it here don't you?'

The sarcasm is totally lost on Ken.

'I'll have to check with the missus.'

For all the world as though they are in some old curiosity shop and his long-suffering, twinkling spouse is busying herself in the back with handicrafts and hand-painted dolls and elves.

'How much are we knocking the gear out for love?' He shouts it so loud that it is entirely possible that the entire North-West Drug Squad can hear.

'Eighty per gram or two hundred quid for three,' the kindly old lady shrieks back from the toy workshop.

'I'll take three.'

'How many sets of works does he get with that then? It's that record producer whizz-kid fella.'

'I don't want any sets of works. I don't use needles. I am not a junkie.' Martin snarls this through gritted teeth. His fists are clenched. He doesn't think of himself as a junkie. He likes to experiment, that is all.

There is perspiration running off his forehead and into his eyes. He wipes it away with the back of his hand in a characteristic manner. He doesn't like the heat. He doesn't like the cold either. It's a constant battle to get exactly the right room and body temperature. He prefers to have the air conditioning turned up full, which a lot of the musicians who he works with misinterpret as him trying to drive them out of the studio. The reality is that opiates increase your body temperature.

He takes the plastic package with its convenient self-seal top, jiggles it around, able to gauge the weight. It is something he has been able to do from a tender age. He is fascinated by weights and measures; by equations and subdivisions. 'That will do,' he concedes.

He hands Big Ken £200 in crisp twenties.

'Not so fast!'

It's an unbelievable line. But it is delivered, with all sincerity, from the doorway of the cramped sitting room by Derek Dodgy, entering the scene.

Dodgy has known Martine, my girlfriend, since she was sixteen, apparently, and has always had a crush on her, which she has refused to reciprocate.

'What the hell is this?' Martin demands incredulously.

Ken shrugs his shoulders docilely; he's probably daydreaming of a prison lunch and a good slop-out.

'Martine owes us hundreds of pounds, possibly thousands, she took a half-kilo off our hands to sell to you lot in Didsbury and Altrincham and all them posh parts round there and we've still not seen a penny, so until we do . . .'

Dodgy is myopic, round, chubby and blobby and entirely without any redeeming features.

But Martin, on this occasion, is a match for him. 'That is my money. These are my drugs, which I have purchased. Comprendez?'

Dodgy looks at Martin with his mean, piggy eyes.

'And who are you?'

'I am the Lord of Disorder. I possess Raw Power. I am the Anti-Christ. I destroy passers-by. I come from Kill City and I am on a mission to kick out the jams motherfuckers!'

Martin roars this speech with absolute conviction. He can do roaring with aplomb when the need arises. Even Big Ken seems momentarily impressed.

Martin has his drugs bag. We back out of the house. Martin waves his hand in the air and for an instant everyone is fooled into believing that he has a gun in his hand.

'Enter the fools, exit the Dragon!'

And we make our getaway.

We stop off at Strawberry Studios so that Martin can do some quick work on a drum track, whilst the 'artists' are not around and able to interfere.

'Can you do out a couple of outrageously huge lines Col? I don't like chasing the stuff in here. The owners get all tetchy and it could set off the fire alarms.'

This seems entirely spurious considering everyone smokes their heads off continuously. Martin has snapped into professional producer mode. He is bringing up a track, listening to something on one earphone, fiddling obsessively with a dial, checking a setting, reaching over and switching on a gizmo. The track comes over the speaker. It is a drier-than-dry drum track, in effect the snare with some tom-tom.

'I just say that faster but slower shit to confuse them,' he confides. 'And it's quite funny.'

I snort up a line. It burns hotly in the nostril and then connects to the brain. It's not something I normally do – snorting smack – it always seems like a waste.

Martin is panning some deep space synthetic sound from left to right over the driving dry percussion track. He drops the sound an octave, and lower. It's only a vibration now. You can feel it in the base of your spine, your lower chakra, and the back of your cranium.

Martin hoovers his scag line voraciously. He pulls up the bass line. I recognise the track. It is an early version of Joy Division's near-pop hit 'Transmission', which he will later rework into one of JD's best-loved and most recognised 'hits' in a spellbinding, clean and reserved production.

Suddenly Martin shuts it all down with one flick of a switch.

The scene is over. The party is finished.

We bundle back into the car.

We drive in silence. Martin is tuned into something deep inside himself.

Martin takes me back to my house. He stares ahead out of the windscreen. I start to clamber out of the Volvo.

'Here, take that, should keep you going.'

He gives me the damaged wrap that contains a good three-quarters of a gram: extraordinary generosity.

'Thanks Martin. I'll see you soon.'

'Yes, see you soon.'

I close the car door, a hefty thunk.

I walk away in silence.

12

What was it about the way Martin Hannett worked in the recording studio that made such an impression on those who worked with him and left such an influential legacy?

He is often described, not least by Tony Wilson, as a genius. CP Lee, I think, got nearer to the mark when he characterised him as an 'obsessive' – obsessed with resonance and reverberation and sound production and prepared to go to any lengths to obtain exactly the right sonic detail. It has often been noted that genius and madness are close bedfellows and there is a thin line between brilliance and lunacy. Maybe Martin walked the tightrope.

Most musicians who worked with him suggested that he was more interested in the machines than the people. 'Sometimes his interest in the gadgets eclipsed his interest in the music that he was supposed to be producing' (Howard Devoto). Apparently, when he was simultaneously recording the Names and Minny Pops (two of Factory Records' European bands) at Cargo Studios, he moved between the two studios or lay on the couch and insisted on multiple takes of each track. What he was doing, in the same way that an obsessive film director like Stanley Kubrick would do, was giving himself the greatest amount of choice when he came to editing and mixing the tracks. He could choose the best bass part from one take and match it to a superior snare drum crash from another.

He was renowned for wrong-footing and surprising the musicians, again in a similar way to a film director looking for the most truthful emotional performance of a particular scene or exact delivery of a line. According to Peter Hook from Joy Division, 'He confused you and made you do something you didn't expect. He was like Pan: he loved making mischief and messing things up.' Hooky also accused Martin of behaving 'childishly' in the studio with his methods of starting at 5 a.m. or turning the air conditioning up, or down, to freezing or sweltering. Martin made it clear that he preferred to work on his own without the interference of the boys in the band.

He was also accused, probably unfairly, of pitting individual members against each other. Derek Bramwood of Strawberry Studios said that you could take a band that had got on brilliantly for twenty years, put them in a studio with Martin Hannett and within five minutes they'd be slashing each other's throats. Martin saw Derek as a bureaucrat, and was never easy around people who he saw as authority figures. (To some extent this was true of his relationship with Tony Wilson.) Derek saw Martin as a liability. It was the old tension between the artistic director and the administrator. There is nothing really to substantiate Derek's claim. In fact the experience, in most cases, seemed to strengthen the groups, if only in the face of eccentric adversity. A Certain Ratio suggested that their experiences with Martin, both in the studio and live in New York, had added to their collective sense of belonging.

ACR were one of the first Factory bands to work with Martin Hannett – first on their *The Graveyard and the Ballroom* cassette-only live/studio blueprint and subsequently on their first 'proper' album, the dub-wise *To Each* . . . Their drummer is scrupulously honest about how difficult he found it, as a drummer, to work with Martin: 'he wanted to record each drum track separately which drove me mad. I'm a funk drummer. You can't do that with a funk drummer'.

Vini Reilly described Martin as 'a big brother' who patiently worked around his idiosyncratic ideas. Patience is not a word often associated with Martin, but it was a quality that he had when it was required and when he felt the ideas were worth teasing out and enshrining. 'He'd pull your brain around until you were in the right frame of mind to produce something special. He'd get you to a zone of creativity where you could create something remarkable, and he was very patient in doing it. He wouldn't stop,' according to Vini.

Martin turned Vini's pastoral guitar doodles into something quite enchanting and beguiling for *The Return of the Durutti Column* with the restrained addition of drum machine shuffles, lubricious bass lines, jazzy inflections and the legendary bird sounds. Initially Vini had been frustrated by Martin's seeming lack of focus and attention, as he endlessly messed around with gigantic boxes of synthesisers and rewound wire, but in the end he conceded that 'The big breakthrough was when Martin made those bird sounds on this big, mad Moog synthesiser'. The mainly instrumental mood music of *The Return of . . .* is entirely at odds with most of his other productions and reveals that he could be versatile and flexible. The straitjacket of the shoe-gazing doom merchants was something that was forced on him, rather than an item he chose to wear.

Bruce Mitchell, who had known him from the early, heady, 60s days, described him as 'good company but badly behaved' and as 'an innovator with a maniacal and meticulous vision'. He embodied the paradox of the artist. Tony Wilson reckons that Martin changed music twice. 'Great producers normally just do one thing . . . the first time he moved music forward was with the digital delay machine which changed drum sounds for ever . . . the second thing he did was that he was the first person to solder wires from the back of archaic computers to keyboards thus making the first modern music.'

He was able to push musicians, particularly fledgling or inexperienced ones, in whatever bizarre ways, and realise their potential. A lot of the bands who worked with him only retrospectively acknowledged his help and vision.

But it is his production of Magazine's third album that is often cited as his technically best, most mature and accomplished work. It is interesting that Howard Devoto, having toiled on *Spiral Scratch* with Martin, should return to employ him on a Virgin Records recording. Magazine had already worked with Mike Thorne on their debut *Real Life* and then with Colin Thurston on their more experimental and commercially less successful follow-up, *Secondhand Daylight*. Both Thurston and Thorne were pretenders to Hannett's throne. They were thirsty thorns in his side.

In 1981 Howard Devoto told the journalist known as Orr: 'Martin moves in his own mysterious way. A lot of musicians find it hard to work with, because he doesn't communicate very well. He sits like Buddha behind the mixing desk, untouchable.' Maybe Martin chose to communicate with those with whom he found it worthwhile and stimulating. He was never one to tolerate fools. That streak in him could be experienced as being arrogant and aloof.

Martin's production of Magazine's *The Correct Use of Soap* is arguably his most restrained. There is little evidence of his trademark digital delay or use of reverb or echo. Possibly it was because the material that he was working with, the songs, were so strong that they needed little in the way of ornamentation. What he did do was frame them and give them space to breathe. Howard Devoto was clear that the reason it is Martin's best production was 'because the band had hands-on involvement on the mixing desk'. This was one of the few projects on which Martin worked with 'real' musicians – Barry Adamson, John McGeoch, Formula himself. The sound palette is comparatively clean and opaque. The album features nu-jazz nuances, jerky rhythms, scratchy guitars, catchy tunes and arid drums underpinning vocalist and lyricist Howard Devoto's musical tales of paranoia, alienation, existential doubt, unrequited love and self-loathing.

Throughout the album, recorded in 1980, it is as though punk had never happened. This album has far more in common with the feel and creativity rush and artistic adrenalin of the glam era – Roxy Music, Be-Bop Deluxe (Bill Nelson's band), Steve Harley's Cockney Rebel, Marc Bolan's T. Rex and David Bowie (especially his albums

Aladdin Sane, *Diamond Dogs* – another study of alienation – and *Young Americans*).

The album opens with 'Because You're Frightened' and the sound is immediately urgent and neurotic, with John McGeoch's guitar close to distortion, but never quite spilling over into Hannett trademark treble disorder. The bass is almost a subliminal rumble in this opening track. Martin perhaps understood the potential and flexibility of the bass more than any other instrument. It was the one he played himself, although he was always self-deprecating in his observations about his own musical ability. Throughout the album Martin features Devoto's vocal with clarity and restraint. On this song the voice seems to travel, at times distant, at times close up, sometimes inside the mix, other times hovering above it. The drum sound is, as always in his oeuvre, clear and vital and well separated. The instruments drop in and out of the mix, but with a subtlety and lightness of touch. It adds to the excitement and uncertainty, reflecting the lyrics. The song finishes on a long fade.

In contrast, the second song 'Model Worker' is Eastern European-sounding, cabaret-style. The piano leads it off. The whole track has a fairground feel, it is going too fast like an out-of-control Hitchcock roundabout, it spins, it is dizzying. At moments it feels as though some of the sounds are falling off the edge of the grooves. The song finally makes a rushed exit, as if the singer/narrator is running off to vomit.

From there, the album slows down, using everything from spare, effective metallic handclaps to klaxons, underscored by a disturbing backing track.

The guitar riff leads the way on the fourth cut, with piano chords and glissandos colouring the scene. It ascends endlessly – a trick that first Buzzcocks, then Magazine had effected with 'Boredom' and then 'Shot by Both Sides'. Martin allows the bass guitar and the bass drum to lock into each other and then to interact, and keeps the vocals dead centre in the mix. The track really opens up halfway through, the backing vocals are ethereal, the instruments beautifully balanced and poised, the whole production becomes widescreen, lush, vertiginous and then is stripped down to further glissando flourishes over bass and drums – sounding like a post-punk modern jazz trio for an interlude.

The seventh track, Magazine's cover of Sly Stone's 'Thank You (Falettinme Be Mice Elf Agin)', is both a deconstruction of the stoned funk of the original and a righteous homage. Barry Adamson, whose bass playing is exemplary at all times and who was to go on to a fruitful, exciting solo career, holds the whole thing down with sly, funky, slap bass. Martin creates the right sense of space, reminiscent this time of Nile Rodgers and Bernard Edwards's production work with the sublime Chic. The white boy guitar sweeps in and out. The keyboards emulate that odd froggy-sounding funk sound favoured by mid-seventies soul bands like Rufus. Other sounds slither in and out of the mix. The guitar starts to build upwards, then cuts out, leaving vocals and percussion to interplay for several bars (in a way that is very similar to Bowie's *Young Americans* blue-eyed soul opus), before the funked-up bass returns and lifts the whole thing along. Martin gives it gaps, space, but nothing too tricksy or fussy.

The songs range from a Roxy Music feel on 'Sweetheart Contract' to funky bass.

At times, the keyboards replicate a rinky-dinky sound; the vocals are double-tracked (Martin rarely uses double-tracking on the album). There are complicated time signatures, which would have defeated lesser musicians. Martin and The Invisible Girls explored them with ease and confidence.

The final cut is the anthemic 'A Song from Under the Floorboards' and in the sequencing of the tracks, as is often the case, the band and producer keep the best for last. It is a panoramic production. There are hooks aplenty: Three of them.

There is the bass part, the keyboard phrase and even the drum pattern, before the big, to-die-for catchy chorus kicks in. The chorus repeats, in pure pop style and as the track, and album, fades, the backing vocals pick up and repeat the word 'habit'.

Although Martin wasn't to work with Magazine directly again, they did send him the recorded tapes of their next, fourth and last studio album, *Murder, Magic and the Weather* (which could very well be a fitting motif for Martin's life), to mix at his leisure, and pleasure, in the familiar surroundings of Strawberry Studios. This could have become the perfect employment for Martin – mixing the recordings without all the hassle and personalities of the in-studio wrangling. Was this an act of generous loyalty by his old friends Devoto and Formula, or did they feel that the tapes lacked presence and the 'magic' of the title without him?

The resultant album is a mixed bag, some might say a retread of *The Correct Use of Soap*, and it lacks the previous record's moments of genuine originality, sparkle and killer hooks. In production terms it seems to lack depth, but this could be due to the fact that Martin had not been present at Trident Studios in London, when the original tracks were recorded and engineered by John Brand in 1981. There was only so much he could do with the master tapes. Many of his signature effects were related to the way he recorded the instruments in the first place and his ambient use of the studio itself.

Nonetheless there are some stand-out moments, not least in the central track 'The Great Man's Secrets' where Martin uses double-tracking and subtle delays on the vocal to great effect, with Barry Adamson's bass again prominently underpinning the procedure. There are some interesting percussive flourishes and squalls of noise and swashes of sound.

On 'This Poison', the band and Martin's mix explore reggae-tinged territory. Martin's obsession with deep dub was becoming more prominent by this point and would culminate in his work with Basement 5 and have an enduring effect on producers right up until the new millennium, especially Adrian Sherwood and his influential On-U label. 'This Poison' also features varispeed voices, curiously reminiscent of early David Bowie ('The Laughing Gnome', 'Space Oddity'), and throughout the album the rinky-dinky keyboards are used, perhaps overused. There are other interesting textural moments including what sounds like the use of a harmonium or indeed a euphonium. Elsewhere, on *Murder, Magic and the Weather*, there is some warm, bubbling bass, and a piping organ sound/setting synthesiser on the 1960s-inflected 'Suburban Rhonda', which is a vignette very much in the style of Ray Davies's songs with The Kinks. There are seaside sounds (Southport beach?) and whirling Wurlitzer. Were the post-war glamour boys, the baby boomers, revisiting the sounds and sensations of their mutual childhoods: a day trip to Kirby or Blackpool?

If Martin's efforts on the two Magazine albums are his most technically accomplished, then perhaps his production of John Cooper Clarke's second album, the brilliantly named *Snap, Crackle and Bop*, is his most imaginative and creative. Surprisingly, perhaps, Martin and Steve cooked up the 'backing tracks' and then John would find some existing lyrics, or indeed write some words, to fit.

There is so much to enjoy; so much wit and invention within the groovy grooves. It is one of the hippest albums ever made, from the hipster title onwards: the cover image of a pair of shades peeping out of a top pocket and the track listing on a white sleeve cuff on the back. It is the perfect marriage between John's witty, erudite, beatnik, literate, punning words and the Hannett & Hopkins sensational soundtracks. In a parallel universe it would have been Number One Album for ever.

It opens with the speed jive of 'Evidently Chickentown', which must contain more expletives than any other track recorded. It motors along, gum-chewing crazily on a manic drum-machine-driven roller-coaster, sounding like an old arthritic steam train. There is a slight delay on the vocals and at odd moments the real drums crash and criss-cross like an accident on the main line. A spectral, spindly guitar hovers over the proceedings, never going anywhere, like a vulture circling and waiting for the carcass. Martin strips the sound down to pure metallic machine before the sudden end. This is the sound of inner-city amphetamine psychosis at its most raw, negative and funny.

'Conditional Discharge' is jokey and has a rock and roll, good-time feel. The drums, courtesy of the brilliant Paul Burgess, who had previously played with Sad Café, are massive. The guitars are provided by stalwart Lyn Oakey and guest Buzzcock Pete Shelley. Most musicians were happy to guest for Martin.

The third track, 'Sleepwalk', is quintessential Martin Hannett brilliance. CP Lee agrees that it is perhaps his greatest production achievement and also feels that it is the way Joy Division should have sounded. The double-tracked bass is a master stroke. It opens with the bass plucked warmly before a sumptuous circling melody appears and a brushed snare drum adds extra tone and colour. It is the sound of sleepwalking. There are Hannett trademark depth-charge drums that startle and unsettle as the keyboard takes central position and holds the whole thing together. The vocals have been subtly treated. It is difficult to identify some of the instrumental colouring. As soon as the track finishes you want to hear it again. You want to return to that uterine, soporific environment. This music is mood-altering. The sound is the drug.

The epic dystopian odyssey that is 'Beasley Street' builds slowly and inexorably. It opens with a disturbed, distorted voice and clatter before that fantastic bass riff kicks in, then glissando flourishes, tambourine and complex drum patterns turn into explosions and then the melody establishes under John's vivid descriptions of life on a north Manchester street in 1980 and by extension the state of the nation.

Like most of Martin's and Steve's compositions, the track is built around the bass and keyboards, as they were their two primary instruments. Martin seldom worked with the more conventional songwriters who build their songs around guitar (often acoustic to commence with) and voice (Lennon/McCartney, Jagger/Richards, Bono/The Edge).

Clarke's voice is recorded to perfection in 'Beasley Street', the merest hint of delay, perfectly placed in the middle of the mix, in the middle of the street. Peripheral noises colour and underline: strange disembodied sounds appear and disappear, like passers-by: a guitar takes up the riff.

'36 Hours', John's tale of prison life, is set to an old-school 12-bar rock and roll romp. There are prominent honky-tonk Hopkins piano, jagged swaggering guitar bursts. The bass pumps, the drums stomp. It captures the echoes and ambience of an enclosed prison. Martin catches the sibilance in John's voice and blends it seamlessly into the mix. It references Presley's 'Jailhouse Rock', the Stones' 'We Love You', 'Riot in Cell Block H' and The Clash's fabulous, rebellious version of 'I Fought the Law'. The arrangement joyously underscores John's comic grotesque images.

This is Martin and his Invisible Girls at their most liberated and jubilant.

But then they are able to totally alter the mood for another masterpiece – 'Belladonna'. This is John's and Martin's ode to heroin. It fades in on a wave of phase before another gorgeous bass line leads the way into the junk yard. A Spanish-sounding guitar, courtesy of wunderkind Vini Reilly, adds texture, tonality and exoticism. The voice is slightly distorted and lowered and recreates the drugged-out drawl of the terminal addict. The soundstage is cavernous, full of gaps, luscious and seductive like opium – 'walking together in the purple snow, to the dying gardens down below'. It ends unexpectedly, like a drug addict's life, mid-bar.

The penultimate track, 'Limbo (Baby Limbo)', has a massive, monstrous soundscape. It is announced by a timpani roll and heralded by blaring horns. Stephanie Formula, who was hired for the one track as she was the only viola player that anyone knew, provides unsettling lines. The drums are subsonic.

The vocals are treated in a similar fashion to 'Belladonna'. There is a palpable air of menace, ugliness and paranoia. It captures the fear of early 1980s Britain's rotting housing estates; encroaching mass drug addiction; the death of dignity. There is almost total disorder in the treble range. It is soaked with Catholic guilt, remorse, black mass.

Martin keeps the bass insistent and threatening. The drum sound grows increasingly unsettling and nearly painful. Horns wail: the sound of decay. It becomes more dissonant, the key changes, 'a stairway to a void', an abrupt end that leaves you hanging: another wonderful wedding of form and content.

In contrast the final track 'A Distant Relation' slides in on a warm plucked bass, late-night drums, wah-wah guitar and tinkling piano: a perfect pastiche. This is junked-up Brompton's Cocktail music. It is lazy, louche and lubricious. Like 'Valley of the Lost Women' (the last track on John's first album, *Disguise in Love*) the pretty melody and arrangement belie the edginess of the lyrics.

There is a subtle guitar break, before the track begins to slightly distort and wail and something shivers, before the prescient final verse, before it shuffles off sleepily and unhurriedly like a good overdose.

Peter Hook once remarked that 'Martin was only as good as the songs he was handed,' and whether that is true or not, perhaps it is true that as the material that he worked with latterly became weaker and more derivative, so his ability to sprinkle his magic became more problematic. Hooky also compared him to a chef, mixing up the ingredients and sprinkling his herbs over the top. Like a chef in his kitchen, Martin was never happier than when looking into the sound booth from behind a gigantic mixing desk, one hand on a fader, the other holding a Marlboro, eyes flicking between dials and humans – in some cases between knobs and knobheads.

13

The time between the making of *Unknown Pleasures* and the creation of *Closer* was less than a year, but it was a period of rapid change for Joy Division, for Ian Curtis and for Martin Hannett. It was also the dawn of a new decade – 1980. Perhaps arbitrarily, we tend to see cultural changes in terms of decades. We refer now to the sixties, seventies and eighties as though we have an implicit common understanding of what that signifies. Often it's a simplistic view of popular history, but it did feel at the end of the seventies as though there could be a new beginning, a fresh start, after the trauma and dislocation and countless changes of that decade. Musically the eighties is now seen as quite different, even separate, from the seventies, and the early eighties is often cited as the time of the New Romantics, ludicrous hairdos, decadence, self-indulgence, Duran Duran, yachts, supermodels, Spandau Ballet, Serious Money, Top Girls, extravagant stylings, big mobile phones, Porsches and cocaine.

Ian's life was becoming more obviously problematic as he tried to deal with the strains, and what he possibly saw as constraints, of having a small girl child and wife and his rising position as front man for a band with a larger and more devoted, and even fanatical, fan base. The fans and music press were waiting eagerly for the next move, the follow-up to *Unknown Pleasures*. Joy Division were beginning to tour away from the safety of North-West England and were venturing into new territories.

Annik Honoré was one of a growing number of European admirers who had been entranced and intrigued by *Unknown Pleasures*; she had travelled over from her native Belgium to witness the band live for herself. She was also there to conduct an interview for the Belgian fanzine *En Attendant*. She first saw Ian and Joy Division on 13 August 1979 at the Nashville in London. After the gig she conducted her interview, which apparently ran to four hours of cassette tape and saw the beginnings of her friendship with Ian, which progressed slowly.

She saw the band play again in Leeds on 8 September. This was a performance by Joy Division at the height of their powers, magnetism and confidence at one of the first major post-punk events, Futurama. The two-day bill also featured Altered Images (with the cute Clare Grogan, fresh from *Gregory's Girl*, bouncing all over the stage), Factory label mates A Certain Ratio, rather tentatively testing the live waters, and the experimental Sheffield-based Cabaret Voltaire, who had already established a connection with Factory through frequent appearances at the Russell Club and contributing two tracks to *A Factory Sample*.

Also playing were the London squat rockers Scritti Politti, in their indie minimalist funk and reggae phase; the Leeds-based politics and punk collective that was the mighty Gang of Four; the Bristol-based Pop Group with their wild permutations, mutant disco, tribal chanting and another charismatic front man in the form of the gangling, pop-Marxist Mark Stewart.

Joy Division were second on the bill to John Lydon's comparatively recent formation Public Image Ltd. They exuded a palpable air of menace and displayed their awesome, dubbed-up tales of alienation, contempt and bile through Jah Wobble's massive bass sound, Keith Levene's eccentric and nerve-shredding guitar doodling and Lydon's trademark snarl and sneer.

Joy Division stole the day at the Futurama festival and converted more worshippers to their brand of tightly wound, introspective, doomy but ferocious musical spirituality, especially in the form of a near-demented Ian Curtis who emanated mystery and magnificence, partly due, in hindsight, to his worsening epileptic condition.

There then followed an extended tour with Buzzcocks and the members of JD, Ian included, were at last able to chuck in their day jobs and concentrate all their time and energies on their baby – the band. Though it would seem that Ian spent less and less time with his *actual* baby, Natalie. She had been born just after the completion of *Unknown Pleasures*, as Martin was mixing it. It was perhaps a near-impossible balancing act: having a young wife and small baby and financial responsibilities on one side and the lure of a glamorous indie rock and roll lifestyle on the other. He was alone in that predicament. None of the other JD chaps had wives or children at that point. Indeed very few of his contemporaries had those kinds of commitments so relatively young.

Soon there followed a first foray into Europe, to the Brussels Plan K club, which was the Belgian equivalent of the Russell/Factory Club and home to Crepuscule Records, a European cousin to the Factory Records label. They appeared on a bill that bizarrely included William Burroughs reading from his books and Cabaret Voltaire. Ian, apparently, was snubbed by Burroughs when he went to talk to him about lyrics and writing.

After the rigours and strains and strangeness of touring and the burgeoning of Ian and Annik's friendship, Joy Division returned to the studio in July 1979 with Martin, to record what should have been a smash hit – the perfect pop-punk-disco of 'Transmission'. It was a track that they had been featuring live for a while and had been previously recorded at Manchester's Central Sound studio, but they returned to the more familiar setting of Strawberry Studios to rework and indeed reinvent it into something altogether more shimmering, more propulsive, catchier and potentially commercial, with its wonderful sing-along hook in Ian's exhortation to 'dance . . . dance . . . dance . . . to the radio'. But although it became, and remains, a cult classic and a defining moment at the end of the seventies and the start of the eighties and represents the bridge between the two decades, it didn't achieve the chart positioning that most people had expected, and indeed were, in Wilson's case, banking on.

The next recording with Martin was the monumental, the monolithic 'Atmosphere', within which is the perfect pairing of Ian's doomed, resigned, mournful lyrics and deepest, most regretful vocals and Martin's huge wall of sound/wall of pain production that harks back to a previous era of The Righteous Brothers, the Walker Brothers, The Ronettes and the awesome Phil Spector himself – another maverick, mythic record producer. Ian enters territory that has seldom been explored within the pop pantheon, apart from by eccentric godlike geniuses such as Scott Walker, Bowie ('Wild Is the Wind') or indeed Jacques Brel. In some ways 'Atmosphere' seems to only feature Ian's voice, so closely miked and yet so distant, so near and yet so far, and Martin's pristine production values, including the use of the legendary giant chimes and huge oceanic washes of synthesised sound and the most massive drum sound that you are ever likely to experience. This could be described as Martin and Ian's relationship encapsulated and preserved for all time within the grooves and gravitas. The haunting 'Don't walk away in silence . . .' becomes a leitmotif for both of their lives and tragic deaths.

The record of 'Atmosphere', backed by 'Dead Souls' in seven-inch format, on the Sordide Sentimental label, housed in a gorgeous sleeve with Anton Corbijn's magnificent, glacial photograph of icy waste and the luxuriant painting by Jamoul, appeared finally in March 1980 with originally only 1,578 copies printed and posted out to the chosen few. It was without doubt a work of art but also another missed opportunity of mythic proportions.

Joy Division returned to the now familiar Strawberry Studios on 24 February 1980 to record a 12-inch version of 'She's Lost Control' that was originally only released in the US and became a dance floor favourite. It was later gloriously covered by mutant-disco diva Grace Jones with the wonderful Chic production team of Nile Rodgers and Bernie Edwards. ('Love Will Tear Us Apart' fared less well in the hands of Paul Young, at the height of his popularity, but it is to his credit that he chose it.)

Martin, in consultation with Wilson and Gretton and Joy Division, decided to try Britannia Row Studios in Islington, north London, as the place to record *Closer*, the eagerly awaited follow-up to *Unknown Pleasures*. In some ways it was an odd decision for a group of fiercely Northern, even Manc-centric, lads who had grown up to mistrust 'poncey' Southerners and conniving cock-er-neys. The studio was owned by Pink Floyd, who a mere couple of years earlier had been reviled by the punks, especially Johnny Rotten, as emblematic of the rock dinosaurs and boring old farts whom the punks wished to destroy. But for Martin, a big fan of early Floyd and their sonic journeys and wayward genius Syd Barrett, it must have had other more resonant connotations.

Britannia Row was booked from 17 March 1980 until the end of the month – less than two weeks to record another masterpiece. The band kipped in two flats on York Street. Annik Honoré had her own place nearby in Parsons Green. Debbie Curtis, literally left holding the baby in Manchester, was unclear at the time as to what the arrangements were and felt that Ian was avoiding her calls. Martin stayed in the neutral surroundings of a hotel and chose to work at night. That suited him just fine.

The London studio felt colder and more clinical than the more familiar Strawberry and this coldness is reflected in the sound and feel of the resultant album, which almost entirely departs from the earlier more ragged, raw, spunkier elements and explores territory that is altogether more sedate and sedated. Bear in mind too that by this point Ian was taking barbiturates as medication for his increasing epilepsy. Barbiturates numb the mind and the emotions. They are the 'downers' of the drug world.

The excitement and camaraderie of the *Unknown Pleasures* sessions seemed absent: the approach was more cerebral, less visceral. Ian was not as obviously in control of the arrangements and orchestrations, so these were left more to Martin. Arguably it is more Martin's album than Ian's, although they continued the close creative partnership that they had explored with 'Atmosphere', with the attention to intimate vocals, existing often in an empty space between the pristinely separated instrumentation. These are songs that seemed to have been recorded in snowstorms, cathedrals, cellars, basements, dungeons, lifts, icebergs. There is little warmth or comfort to be had and indeed the song sequencing charts a descent from the opening mania of 'Atrocity Exhibition' and manic power pop of 'Isolation' to the auto-depressive depths of the final tracks, 'The Eternal' and 'Decades'.

Outside of the studio, there was little or no contact between Ian and Martin. Ian was seeing more of Annik during the daytime or scouring the shops and market stalls with chum Genesis P-Orridge of Throbbing Gristle notoriety, on the lookout for obscure objects, bizarre ephemera or arcana. Martin was holed up in his hotel, sleeping through the day, eating room service snacks, settling for lower-grade, impure, street heroin to feed his habit as he was unfamiliar with the rip-off drug dealers of central London. One night he drove the 250 miles from London up to Manchester, at 5 a.m. after finishing a long session, came round to my house at 10 a.m., scored in Bury by 1 p.m. (first thing you learn is you always gotta wait) and drove back down to t'Smoke in the afternoon. He was even resorting to alcohol to take the edge off his withdrawals.

But he was focused on the task at hand. This would be his meisterwerk. Other groups seemed to be flocking to work with him and he still had the enthusiasm and appetite to explore and experiment. After all this was what he had wanted to do all of his life, since he began his precious record collection and listened closely to the sonic details and artistic signatures of the artists and producers whom he favoured.

Relationships between band members were becoming strained. They were aware of Ian's escalating health problems due to his epilepsy and of his growing involvement with Annik, who described what she heard of the *Closer* sessions as 'sounding like Genesis'. Ian was perhaps beginning to pay too much attention to her opinions. He was starting to panic and to feel that the sessions would have to be radically remixed. This doubt had not been present at the earlier *Unknown Pleasures* sessions. He was losing control.

Bernie Sumner recalled in Mick Middles and Lindsay Reade's book *Torn Apart*: 'I remember being at Britannia Row and asking Ian whether he was feeling all right because he'd been acting strangely for days, and he said, "It feels like I'm caught in a whirlpool and I'm being sucked under water."'

Closer was eventually released to almost unanimous glowing reviews and critical acclaim, and though there was some dissent regarding Martin's production, most reviewers acknowledged the ground-breaking nature and startlingly original sound of the album. Dave McCullough in *Sounds* magazine used the phrase 'dark strokes of gothic rock' to describe the feel of the record. It was undoubtedly a giant leap, not only for Joy Division, but for the through line of rock music, in the broadest sense, and it still casts a shadow over a whole range of genres, groups and artists, be they new goths, emo or indie.

Is it just with the benefit of hindsight, in retrospect, that we experience the Joy Division album *Closer* as prophetic and prescient? The album starts with 'Atrocity Exhibition': 'this is the way, step inside', into a soundscape of industrial distorted guitars, de-snared toms and a repetitive bass riff that seems prepared to go on for ever and lead us God knows where. In the second track, 'Isolation', the voice is distanced from the music, separate and alone as mechanistic electronic drums and chorused bass drive the song towards a punitive precipice.

On the second side we are in a different place. Somewhere warmer, a lonely place doubtless. The vocal delivery is softer, almost falsetto, very Jim Morrison, coming from the periphery of consciousness. The lyrics themselves are seemingly gentler too with talk of heart and soul and slow-burning fires. The landscape is parched, barren, deserted. But as with all deserts there is an ominous beauty to be discovered in the vast emptiness. Martin saw all this internal post-apocalyptic landscape and helped to translate it into an external soundscape with chorused bass playing high melodic lines (something he favoured in his own bass playing), chiming, cascading Rickenbacker guitar strums referencing the Byrds, and military snare snaps counterpointing the dreamy quality – a reminder of the external, hostile, threatening world.

More and more as the album progresses the bass guitar becomes the lead melodic instrument, tuning itself with our heartbeats and innermost hopes and fears. Martin treated it with chorus and a short delay making the sound paradoxically both warmer and more alienated. It creates inevitability, which is something that depressives often talk about – a compulsion towards their own termination. It can seem like the only possible outcome and within that there is a tragic solace to be had.

Ian sings of having to go to extraordinary lengths and looking beyond the daylight, or is it danger?, and his voice takes on an urgency and desperation. There is the dirgelike trudge of 'The Eternal' – the ultimate pop suicide song, a good choice for any premature post-adolescent funeral. A long drone on a Mellotron, an electronic snare with a long digital reverb, heavy use of percussive sound effects create the ambience of stasis. Ian's voice is disembodied, off the planet. After Ian dies, Martin will remember doing the vocal track, just the two of them and an engineer in the middle of some dark, starless night. Some time between three and four in the morning – the hour of the wolf. It is the time when most people are born and die; when the body is at its lowest ebb. Martin was well informed on the subject of the body's internal (at times infernal) clock, what has been described as the clock of the heart.

Years later Mick Middles would write: 'Ian's studio technique had certainly improved. He'd developed an ability to latch onto the melody and write his way into the heart of the song, at times climbing right onto the feel, as if the songs had been waiting for him . . .'

Martin had undoubtedly played a large part in that learning process. He had nurtured and encouraged Ian. He believed in the boy. Ian had looked up to him, admired him, respected him, and perhaps even worshipped him. Martin intuitively understood what Ian was trying to express through his anguished, sometimes oblique, lyrics. He knew, through his childhood religion, through his own warped spirituality, through his chemical research, the profound feelings of despair, and the search for redemption.

For Martin, it was a return to his affection for the doomed front men and women of an earlier generation. It is what is most vibrant and exciting and truthful at the heart and soul of popular music. It is rock and roll religion.

But the *Closer* sessions were to be the last ones that Ian did with Martin.

In February 1980 Ian attempted suicide and self-mutilated. Stephen Morris remembers that 'He talked about it as though he'd gone through some strange religious experience.' The boundaries between the internal and the external were blurring – often a side effect of pro-longed barbiturate usage and an after-effect of epileptic fits, which historically were often linked to ecstatic religious experiences. Back with Debbie in Manchester on Easter Monday, 7 April, Ian took an overdose of phenobarbital tablets and was taken to hospital where his stomach was pumped. He had written a suicide note, but survived.

During the night of Saturday 17 May/Sunday 18 May 1980 Ian eventually took his own life. He was 23.

Ian, and the rest of Joy Division, had been scheduled to fly to America, for their first and potentially career-defining tour there, on Monday 19 May. He had stayed with Tony Wilson and Lindsay Reade for a while previously, but then had moved into his parents' house.

At about 11 a.m. on the morning of Sunday 18 May, Debbie found his body hanging, lifeless, from an old pulley that had been used for drying clothes. By the time she discovered him, the rope had broken, cutting his neck, and his corpse seemingly knelt on the bare floor, as if in supplication.

Legend now has it that the night before he must have returned to his little family's home, drunk too much on top of his medication, watched a Werner Herzog movie on video, listened to Iggy Pop's *The Idiot* and then hanged himself.

Once Joy Division's manager Rob Gretton had been told about the suicide there was a flurry of phone calls to inform those closest to Ian – including Martin Hannett. Martin said that his initial reaction was one of shock, followed by anger. But many of the people who knew Ian weren't so shocked by the grim news. As Vini Reilly commented: 'I was waiting for the phone call and I wasn't remotely surprised.' A slew of lurid stories about the event proliferated, adding an even more gruesome note to the already tragic events.

There is never a simple explanation for a suicide and there are a number of theories, some of them conflicting, about what led to Ian's. It seems to me that a huge factor would have been Ian's intake of prescribed barbiturates for his epilepsy, combined with alcohol and the pressures closing in on him. Perhaps even the thought of the imminent trip to the USA was filling him with anxiety.

But Debbie Curtis is certain that he had not been drinking and had in fact stopped his medication. She told me in 2007, 'There were no drugs prescription or otherwise on his person or in the house . . . no one ever mentions the dangers of ceasing medication suddenly and without discussion with a doctor. That night he did consume vast quantities of coffee, which, coupled with the absence of his prescription, would have been enough to cause the agitation and the anxiety.' Like the myths surrounding Martin, those surrounding Ian Curtis may also have replaced the truth.

A number of friends and family paid their last respects to Ian in a chapel of rest.

Martin chose not to visit the body of his young friend; neither did he attend the funeral or the wake. It was as if his younger self had died. His grief, which continued for many years after the event, and arguably right up until his own death, was as much about his own dying inner self, and increasing despair, as it was about Ian Curtis. Perhaps Martin had seen some possible redemption through the words and voice and shamanic performances of his youthful protégé. With Ian gone, there was no escape route, no way through to the other side.

As Tony Wilson told me in 2006: 'Martin would appear at my door, years later, and stand sobbing in the rain. He never really got over it. He never really came to terms with it. I think he felt guilty, as though he could have helped Ian.'

Ian's body was cremated on Friday 23 May 1980. It was a family affair. Factory Records held their own wake at their offices on Palatine Road, which had seen the birth of so many young careers and aspirations and discs. They weren't sure how to commemorate a death, but this would only be the first of several untimely deaths over the years to come. The mood was subdued, almost repressed. Northern males aren't renowned for openly expressing their emotions. There was a feeling of uncertainty about what would happen next and if this would be the end of Factory Records and budding careers. Some of the women present, including Lindsay Reade, did allow their emotions to show, but their tears seemed to be an affront to the toughing-it-out males. The Sex Pistols' recent film *The Great Rock 'n' Roll Swindle*, charting the rise and fall of punk rock as orchestrated by Malcolm McLaren, was shown at the occasion, a strange choice perhaps. There were plates of 'posh' triangular sandwiches and nibbles, prepared by Alan's girlfriend who owned a bistro in Didsbury.

Paul Morley later commented that 'It was a very, very weird mixture of energy . . . the atmosphere was deeply traumatised . . . but everyone was trying to cover it up.'

14

This is just perfect, just peachy cream. Here is Martin, the Young Man, in a spiritualist church in Ashton-under-Lyne, a grimy satellite town of north Manchester, only a bloodied stone's throw away from the killing fields of the Moors murderers. His head is still full of the graphic images, the unexpected violence and the grief of Ian Curtis's suicide. He has an aching in his chest, dry heat at the back of his throat. He has a deep sense of his own mortality and a premonition of his own death. The two thick lines of Iranian smack that he snorted before leaving his flat cannot quiet or quell the chattering, impish devils or lessen the ferocious feeling of foreboding and impending doom.

Ian's lyrics resound and rebound around his head in that booming, broken voice that he had captured so well. He tries instead to focus on the absurdity of the situation. Martine Helene and I are getting married.

I met Martine at the tail end of 1978 in the Arndale Shopping Centre in central Manchester, when I was in the process of putting together my very own glam-post-punk band, The Roaring 80s. I had found a great Velvets-obsessed guitarist – Simon Taylor – and a whizz-kid/rich kid bass player with lots of flashy equipment and bright ideas – John Hurst. We were in search of a drummer, as most bands were in those days, and we briefly had Steve Brotherdale occupying the drum stool, as he had done for Joy Division (who he dissed at every opportunity). We had some songs that Simon and I had written in his attic whilst I was nodding out over a microphone, a basic amplifier, a twenty-quid deal and his gorgeous cream Fender Telecaster – 'Apparently', 'Song of Gloom', 'Normal', 'Cute in a Suit', 'Hard Core' and 'Tunnel Vision'. We had some covers – 'I'm a Believer', 'Paint It Black', 'Sweet Jane' and of course 'Heroin'.

So it was that John Hurst and I were in the Arndale Centre, our purpose being to look on the noticeboard of Virgin Records for possible drummers. That's how we bumped into Martine and her friend (sweet) Jane. Martine was 19, drop-dead gorgeous in a Debbie Harry kind of way. She had been using, I soon found out, regularly since she was 15 when it had all gone wrong when her family had left their idyll in the Lancashire countryside. They had moved into grimy old Ashton and her parents had got divorced, and she had had to leave the horses, who were the only real love of her life. She was the oldest of five – a younger sister and three younger brothers. She had secrets.

John and I met her and Jane that night in a gay bar in Manchester, near Piccadilly Station, and they came back to my house in Withington. We drank plenty of cheap pink wine and we took lots of speed, which at that moment was her preferred drug – she was trying to stay away from narcotics. We listened to Bowie and Lou Reed and Roxy Music. John and Jane slept downstairs and Martine slept on my floor and told me some story about how she had spent the previous night on a random guy's roof after she had decided he was a twat and had escaped out of his bedroom window. I should have realised then. In the middle of the night she clambered up onto the end of my bed and curled up there like a pussycat, but that's as far as we went on our first date – we were curiously moralistic.

We saw each other fairly regularly for the next year and she stayed more and more at my house before we eventually fell into living together. This is how she met Martin. He seemed to find her amusing and charming and delightful in a way that I could understand. She could be very funny; she had a natural appreciation of music, she looked fantastic, she was sexy as hell. She was a rock chick before the term had been invented. She liked him a great deal.

On this day, our wedding day, Martine is near the end of her pregnancy. In fact she will give birth the following Saturday, in the godless surrounds of a south Manchester maternity ward, to a baby who will become Martin's godson. There will be a special unit standing by in case the baby is born addicted to heroin. She only realised that she was pregnant at six months. One of the side effects of opiate addiction is the cessation of menstrual periods, so it becomes difficult to notice any subtle changes in the body, like pregnancy.

I have gallantly offered to marry Martine, although not foolish or naive enough to think I could, ever, make an honest woman of her. It will, however, stop the Social Services from taking the infant into care. I own a terraced house in suburban Withington and, on paper at least, have the air of middle-class respectability. She, on the other hand, is on probation, on heroin and on the game.

Martin scans the occupants of the dowdy, wooden church hall, like something from a previous century, like something from Arthur Miller's *The Crucible*. The place is poisoned by suppressed sexuality, toxic shame and angry guilt. All dressed up to kill, with nowhere to go. These are the same miserable bastards who twenty years later will try and convert Martine Helene to their dreadful brand of born-again insanity. These are the same spiritually impoverished buggers who will crowd round her coffin like death watch beetles.

I am in the midst of them, a speed freak, stick-insect-thin, rotten Bowie clone with my chopped, crazy-colour-red, sticky-up hair. I am dressed for the, remarkably odd, occasion in a white linen suit with a pink carnation in the lapel and a scarlet silk shirt, just to add a touch of colour to the otherwise monochrome proceedings. I have injected myself with such a ridiculously large amount of amphetamine sulphate that I am, possibly visibly, shaking.

Martine Helene is wearing a matching outfit, but at the moment she is absent. She is in the outside toilet (the 'netty') with her dissolute bridesmaid Fleur. They are in the toilet making last-minute adjustments to their maquillage and Martine Helene is trying to find an uncollapsed vein to stick the blunt needle into. She has more track marks than the entire British rail network. Fleur is cooing into Martine Helene's ear like some deranged lovebird. Fleur's veins (a post-Velvets song title right there) are so thin that she has to 'skin pop'. The exotic combinations of the 'big day', the strong drugs and the proximity of the lovely, heavily pregnant bride-to-be have got her close to orgasm. She's a funny one is our Fleur.

My dear old Mum Dorothy has unexpectedly turned up for the romantic occasion, even though she despises Martine Helene with a murderous passion bordering on the psychotic. She has made a real effort with a new spray-on hairdo, a natty light blue suit and a rictus smile. She will, later on in the day, detect a deathly 'aura' around Martin. She believes, absolutely, in a very literal, unforgiving reincarnation philosophy.

At Martin's side is his girlfriend Suzanne O'Hara, trying to suppress an asthma attack. She has a similar look to Martine Helene, although she is taller and skinnier.

Other members of this cracked cast include Martine Helene's parents, who are in the midst of an acrimonious divorce, and the spiritualist minister, Albert Scrimshaw, who drinks whisky mixed with sterilised milk to steady his nerves and presumably to keep the spirits from the other side at bay.

Martin is overcome by a wave of grief and fatigue. He sits down on one of the old wooden benches at the rear of the church hall. Suzanne is unable to suppress a coughing fit, so she heads out of the door for a fag. She is wearing a thin, brightly patterned, pop-arty dress that clings greedily to her slender, slinky frame. Albert Scrimshaw eyes her lustily and winks salaciously at Martin, as if to imply that they are somehow complicit in their lechery and debauchery.

Martin looks away in disgust. The feelings of sorrow and remorse grip his innards and his throat, like a rusted metal glove, to the extent that he doubles up, arms crossed, clinging to his sides. Was there something he should have said to Ian, some meaningful heart-to-heart that they could have had during the recording of *Closer*? Were there some words of comfort and counsel that he could have offered as they sat side by side, during the hour of the wolf, trying to achieve just the right amount of echo on the vocals? After all it was obvious to everyone that Ian's respect for Martin bordered on hero worship. But Martin has never been good with advice: he is known for his legendary silences, and extended pauses, in the recording studio and his wry, dry humour elsewhere.

'Don't walk away . . . in silence.'

Ian's doomed voice intoning the premonitory lyrics fills his head again. The drugs aren't working like they used to; like they're supposed to. It already takes more and more to silence the chattering, vengeful, spiteful, little bastard devils that inhabit his conscience and his consciousness.

Suddenly, thankfully, there is activity. Albert Scrimshaw begins to process down the aisle to the front of the 'church', flanked by two elderly death watch widows. Another wizened old crow strikes up a few discords on the wheezing organ.

It sounds like some dreadful version of Martin's recent masterpiece 'Atmosphere'. Martin looks up. It's like the scene towards the end of *The Graduate*: all he sees are angry lips mouthing accusations.

'Where is Martine? What is she doing in there?'

'I bet she's collapsed . . . again.'

'She's with that stupid, stupid girl.'

'She's supposed to be getting married. This is meant to be her Big Day.'

I look around, searching the hideous, noxious hall for my friend, hoping he's made it to 'the gig', feeling that only he can rescue and support me in this my hour of need. Then I see his hallowed head of dark brown curls. He looks up and manages that faint, enigmatic smile: a male Mona Lisa. I am saved, for Martin is, and always will be, my BEST MAN.

So . . . not much later, the wedding service as such having been mercifully short, if not sweet, the major players reconvene at my terraced house in suburban Withington. At this point, it still has all its windows intact and no minor gangsters living in the back bedroom. Within a year, this will no longer be the case. There will be boarded-up windows, no leccy, shooters in knicker drawers, sawn-offs under the urine-soaked mattress, baby on the 'at risk' list, bent building society books, rats with rickets . . .

Martine's parents disappear into the kitchen, which has been extended recently and sports a pinewood table and chair set, which will be sold off to pay drug debts within the next twelve months. At this moment, though, it bears 'eats', 'nibbles' and even some drinks.

The rest of us gather in the front room. Martin, Suzanne, Martine and I, Fleur, my dear old Pinteresque mum Dorothy, my sister's boyfriend Phil who has appeared late from the windswept wastes of Newcastle and my ex-girlfriend Louise in her legendary skintight leopardskin trousers, who missed the whole bizarre ceremony by going to the wrong church.

We all stand, crammed together.

'I'll help Martine's dad and . . .' My mother struggles, never able to remember Martine's mum's foreign-sounding name.

'Me Mum,' Martine says. 'If they haven't killed each other by now. Are there any bread knives out? Better stow them out of sight.'

'Out of sight, out of mind,' Phil laughs, as he's immaculately stoned on best Moroccan, as ever.

'Out of Our Heads!' Fleur squawks, quoting a Rolling Stones album title in an attempt to ingratiate herself with Martin who she has decided is gorgeous and, more interestingly, possibly has oodles of spare cash as he's some sort of record producer-type bloke, according to the bride.

Martin sits on the green settee. Suzanne arranges herself modishly on one side of him. Fleur, like a shabby post-war glamour girl, crams herself on his other side. I perch on the narrow arm of my new wife's armchair in a vain attempt to be husbandly and protective. Phil slouches himself down into the other chair and begins to roll an unfeasibly large joint.

'I need a hit,' Martine announces.

'Oh yeah. Here you are. Congratulations. May all your troubles be small ones,' Martin says, fishing out a nicely wrapped package.

We have asked, from our friends, for presents of only Class A drugs. Martin has generously provided us with two grams of Oldham's best on this special occasion. Martine and Fleur have already demolished the quarter-gram that the bridesmaid had managed to gift us.

'Thanks . . . that's really nice of you,' Martine says cheerily as if she's received a teasmade or a set of best crockery.

'It's what we've always wanted,' I deadpan.

'It's the least we could do,' Martin grins.

I am loath to hand the gift-wrapped present to my beloved, as I know she will use most of it immediately. Luckily I am saved by Martine's dad entering jovially and announcing 'Grub's up!' in his gruff Lancashire burr.

'Sounds good to me,' I offer, trying to enter into the jollity of the occasion, but also keen not to be left alone with my newly wed wife in case she starts demanding ownership of the two grams of scag.

Martine's focus is entirely on the two grams in my white trouser pocket. She is even considering jamming her hand into the pocket, giving my balls a none too tender squeeze and fishing the gear out.

Suzanne, having tried and failed to get Martin's attention, leaves. She is never comfortable around hard drug use, nor is she comfortable around working girls like Martine. She mistrusts their motives, quite rightly, and she is wary of Martin's interest in them, which could border on fatal fascination. He likes the dark side: Suzanne doesn't. She doesn't manage to storm out, more of a minor squall.

'I'm going to get some nosh,' Martine announces, unexpectedly.

The combination of a massive heroin habit and the latter stages of pregnancy means that when she does eat, which is rarely, she eats the most bizarre combinations of food (chips covered in jam, peanut butter and tomatoes, oranges and pickled onions).

Martine's dad, the proud father-in-law, follows his daughter and her peachy bridesmaid into the kitchen.

'I think they've had a spat,' my mum hints, indicating the retreating back of dad-in-law, as he exits.

We are all rather confused by the use of the somewhat archaic word 'spat'.

'I'll see what there is,' Phil mumbles, managing to push himself up, intent on smoking his spliff, but considerate enough not to do it in front of his girlfriend's mum. Louise follows him.

So that leaves me, Martin and Mum.

'You don't seem well,' Mum states flatly, squinting intently at the peripheral space around his head. 'Your aura is most unusual.'

Martin is intrigued.

'Why? What can you see?'

'It's difficult to decipher . . . there are . . . flecks of darkness,' she tells him gently.

Martin is slightly alarmed by this oracular pronouncement.

'How do you mean? Where?'

He peers out the corner of his eye, hoping to catch sight of these dark-hued harbingers.

'They are in amongst the purple, the yellow and the . . . orange.'

This is rapidly turning into a Jimi Hendrix song; I half expect to hear a flanged-out guitar solo.

'They're moving around.'

'Bloody hell – excuse my French. Moving around: is that good or bad?'

'It's just what they do. They don't like to stay still.'

Martin stands up, as if he has a swarm of luminous, exotic insects circling his head. It's another 'howl-round' moment. I jump up too, in case he needs help.

'Shall we . . .'

I know exactly what he means: heroin users' telepathy.

'I didn't mean to worry you, Martin,' my mum says, 'it's just very noticeable. I thought you should know.'

I move ahead of him towards the door and the promise of narcotic relief.

Martin looks down at my mother. She is frail; frailty was her constant state.

She reads the question in his anxious eyes.

'There's nothing I can do about it, is there? The flecks of darkness, they'll take over eventually won't they? There will be no deep purple, no purple haze, no mellow yellow, no agent orange.'

Martin's voice is level, but I can hear the foreboding within it. My sweet mother doesn't want to upset the young man, but neither can she lie.

Martin turns away and follows me into the corridor. There are tears in his eyes.

'She's right, you know. I don't how long. I don't know how. Probably not even an overdose. That's the problem with not shooting up – you can't even look forward to a good old-fashioned overdose.'

The shared gallows humour kicks in again: our salvation and our curse.

We find ourselves upstairs in what we could, laughingly, refer to as the master bedroom. I produce the generous wedding gift.

Martin produces some clean tin foil and a home-made pipe – some rolled-up cardboard. It's one that he has made earlier.

'Shall I put some music on?'

It's a standard question.

The album on the top of the pile is Brian Eno's *Before and After Science*. It is an album recorded in 1977, in some ways an early post-punk record, although Eno had cleverly sidestepped punk itself. It is a record that Martin and I both appreciate.

I place the stylus on the track 'Here He Comes', which seems entirely apt. We always found the soundtrack for our lives; the song to suit the second. Martin admires Brian Eno and his vertical colour of sound, his theories of chance and random precision. Martin is never less than generous in his praise of other creative artists and iconoclasts.

'You keep that for later. It's a wedding present. I've got some good Thai gear.'

We like to see ourselves as connoisseurs of smack. It has evolved into a running joke with references to fictional scag such as Cambodian Clay, Vietnamese Victory, even Romanian Rubble, which would describe any rough stuff of dodgy, dubious quality. In reality most of it comes from Rochdale, Guide Bridge, Oldham, Moseley, Chorley and other godforsaken places in rainswept Lancashire.

We chase meandering lines of Thai Tiger, holding the narcoleptic fumes deep down in our perishing lungs, like swimmers trying to break the record for staying underwater without oxygen. The instrumental section with its melodic Moog, the ethereal cadences of the Yamaha CS-80, the harmonics of the bass guitar washes over us and sweeps us away.

The melancholic moment is interrupted by the noisy entrance of the two women. They fall into the room, clinging onto each other in a manner that suggests scatological, schoolgirl, stoned idiocy and lush lipstick lesbianism in equal, intoxicating, measures.

'We wondered where you were,' Martine overenunciates.

It's a vocal mannerism that heroin users adopt to break up the mumbles and mutters that are their usual stock-in-trade. Their mutual focus is firmly on the opened package of golden brown opiate, that lies as if on display in an upmarket jeweller's boutique. If their eyes could widen they would, but their pupils are so permanently dilated that it is unthinkable.

I exhale more acrid, narcotic smoke. It is a worrying feature of chasing the dragon that you seem to go on exhaling fumes for far longer than you inhaled them. Perhaps it is smoky slivers of your soul that you expire, until you are left with none: running on empty, spiritually bankrupt.

I sidle and slide over to the record player, which is top of the range, state of the art, high fidelity. I backtrack to the previous cut on the Eno album. 'King's Lead Hat' is a better soundtrack to this new chaotic scene. Martine scrabbles around in her knicker drawer, which is always the hiding place for used sets of works. Fleur crouches on her haunches, rests her elbows on Martin's knees and chases the trail of smoke as he heats it from beneath with his Zippo. It is an act of extraordinary intimacy and simultaneously, paradoxically, one of total indifference.

'Can you put on that "Fade to Grey", Visage thingy?' Martine requests.

'Fuck me, that is frigging good,' Fleur announces as she breathes out plumes of smoke and reveals her true, faded, colours.

'I told you. Titanic Thai: you sink like a stone to the bottom of the ocean.'

We also like to dream up our own advertising slogans that would go with each exotic brand.

Martine discovers a comparatively unused works. There is a charred spoon, a glass of murky water and a black leather belt permanently available on the little stool next to the bed.

'I think my mum and dad are about to have an almighty bloody barney,' she tells us, as she prepares her hit efficiently and quickly. It's a technique that junkies unconsciously develop to divert attention away from what they are doing, from the greedy amount of gear that they are consuming.

She scoops some brown powder with her wedding ring finger.

'That's a lovely wedding ring you got there my love,' Martin observes, using one of his older character from *Coronation Street* impersonations: a Rovers Return regular.

'Twenty quid from Ratners,' she informs him.

'A bargain,' he muses.

She laughs: a genuine laugh of genuine amusement.

'I wanted to nick one, but he wouldn't let me,' she confides as she mixes the potent powder into the water.

'What do you expect?' I join in, coming back over. 'I'm trying to make an honest woman of you.'

Martine breaks open a cigarette tip to use as a makeshift filter. Martin watches her with fascination. She hands me the loaded works. I hold it for her as she removes her white bridal jacket. Her top is bright red. Her breasts are larger than usual due to her advanced state of pregnancy. She slaps the skin behind her elbow. It looks like the Leeds intersection.

She sees a possibility. She ties the belt tightly.

I hand her the syringe.

'Got you, you bugger,' she announces.

It's a minor victory, a tawdry triumph.

She slides the end of the spike into the saucy little vein that seems to have appeared from nowhere. She pulls the plunger back carefully. The blood flows back, opens like a rose in the barrel. She pushes the plunger home; the liquid shoots up the dropper's neck. Her head jerks back, the tendons on her neck strain, her mouth opens wide, then she bites hard down onto her lower lip, as the rush hits her and infuses her bloodstream. It's like watching her orgasm. Then she shudders, immediately scratches her left shoulder as the glorious heat radiates within her.

'I'd better go and see what me parents are up to,' she announces, hardly missing a beat. 'Before they kill each other.'

She nudges Fleur, who has sprawled out on the dark blue threadbare carpet, with her foot.

'Hey, Fleur, you coming with me or are you going to lie around up here all day? It's me frigging wedding day you know, you lazy cow!'

'All right, all right, I'm coming,' Fleur mumbles.

The bouncy bridesmaid gets up, modestly smoothes down her white dress, smiles sweetly at the two men and then dutifully follows the bride. She is truly the maid of dishonour.

Contrary to all received wisdom, and however short-lived, there is a warmth and camaraderie and cosiness between us.

15

In late 1980, Rob Blamire and Pauline Murray from the North-East punky new wave band Penetration came down to Manchester to work with Martin Hannett on an album that would eventually become the groundbreaking, though seldom heard, *Pauline Murray and the Invisible Girls* (not the most inspiring title ever). Pauline had one of the best rock voices of all time, punk or otherwise.

It would be an interesting visit.

To save money they are staying with Martin and Suzanne in the infamous Hannett Hotel. Martin has been unable to meet them at Manchester Victoria Station, so like a couple of hicks from the sticks they've put their pennies together and got a Manc cab to Didsbury. They stand on the doorstep with their bags stuffed with new wave clothes, songs in school notebooks, Rob's guitar in a shiny new black case. She is wearing a red headband and black leather trousers. Rob is very tall and handsome. They make the perfect new wave couple.

Martin opens the door wide, playing the part of mine host.

'Well, hello there.'

They have met on one previous occasion, backstage at Rafters, when Martin congratulated them on writing 'one of the best pop-punk 45s ever', 'Don't Dictate', and on their superb cover version of Patti Smith's 'Free Money'. He announced 'I am going to work with you,' in a very loud and somewhat grandiose manner. He seems significantly chubbier now than he was then.

'Follow me!'

They drag their valises behind him.

'This will be your chamber,' he announces majestically, returning to the Grand Guignol persona that he adopted on their previous meeting. He ushers them into the downstairs boudoir. It has been spring-cleaned and aired, and fresh laundry is evident.

'A glass of champagne?'

Pauline nods keenly. Perhaps the gothic tales of debauchery and decadence have been grossly exaggerated.

They follow Martin again as he sweeps into the kitchen. The young punk rocker couple stop in the doorway in amazement.

The kitchen is full of a maze of giant test tubes, glass containers, pipes, Bunsen burners, pipettes, sealed jars. Water is actually bubbling in some of the tubes.

The kitchen has been converted into an experimental drugs laboratory.

'Welcome to the cabinet of Doctor Hannetti. I am searching for the secret of Life,' Martin informs them gleefully. 'Soon every recording studio in the universe will be mine!'

He cackles manically.

Thus begins their visit.

The recording sessions themselves were slow and laborious and Martin, in the studio, seemed to adopt a Stalinist persona, pushing Pauline for yet another and yet another and yet another vocal take until she felt she couldn't bear it any more. Was it a conscious ploy on Martin's part to get the best performance out of an artist, in the same way that the film-maker Stanley Kubrick would endlessly retake scenes in an attempt to break his actors down and reveal a truthful performance? Was he hoping to push Pauline to some hitherto undiscovered place and release a primal vocal style that she had previously been unaware of? Or was he just crabby and bored and slightly withdrawing from his Caligari medicine?

Graciously, at the time, Pauline said in an interview with *NME*: 'He just seemed to have the knack of putting everything in the right setting. He works in a totally different way to any other producer we've recorded with. He doesn't even replay the songs on the tape very much. He has it all in his head . . . he's a weird bloke but we work very well with him. I had been stuck in a rut and I needed someone like that to show me some sort of light. Martin was just the right person.'

So had Martin showed her 'some sort of light'? By this time his grasp on his professional work was beginning to loosen and his addictions had begun to tighten their stranglehold on him. Outside of the studio he was aloof, enigmatic to the point of indecipherable, and invariably very, very stoned.

The plan had been to make a 'commercial' album that would relaunch Pauline Murray's musical career after the demise of Penetration. This was at the time of Debbie Harry's glorious ascendant with the divine Blondie; of Chrissie Hynde reinventing herself from a rock chick *New Musical Express* journalist into a rock goddess with her Pretenders persona. Toyah and Hazel O'Connor were waiting in the new wave wings. Even Patti Smith was having some wider, public, commercial success with her take on Bruce Springsteen's 'Because the Night' and the attendant album *Easter*.

The resultant *Pauline Murray and the Invisible Girls* album, truthfully, is something of a curate's egg. It is never sure whether it is electro-pop or experimental lite; metallic disco or mutant dance. For a record that supposedly showcases the lead singer, the voice is often mixed well down and at points is nearly swamped by the keyboard-led instrumentation. Pauline is sometimes left struggling to find a tune in the midst of all the musical arrangements and multi-tracking. When it, or Martin, allows itself to break free more it shines, as demonstrated in the doomier tones of 'Drummer Boy' or the darker hues of 'Mr X'.

Whatever the intentions had been, Pauline and Rob returned to the safe haven of Newcastle exhausted and confused. And although the album, released appropriately on the Illusive label, put in a brief appearance at number 25 on the national album chart, it didn't propel

Pauline into the world of new wave superstardom. It would be a while before she was able to process the experience and write again.

It had been a weird trip.

16

After Ian's death Joy Division, posthumously, enjoyed their biggest chart success with the anthemic 'Love Will Tear Us Apart'. With its gorgeous mournful melody, Ian's resigned tuneful croon, catchy synth lines, sing-along chorus, ambivalent meaning and mythic status, it is still the one song that most people know from Joy Division's repertoire. *Closer* was also released in America to a deal of acclaim and reasonable sales and in Britain it gained enormous respect, matching commercial success and legendary eminence.

Factory Records initially suffered after Ian's sudden death. There was a plethora of new bands, often seen as grey and post-industrial and miserable for the sake of it, whereas what was catching the public's – and indeed the in-crowd's – imagination was something far more colourful, danceable and upbeat. The early incarnations of Ultravox, Spandau Ballet, Culture Club were appearing and the whole emerging funk/punk New Romantics and the accompanying club scene was beginning. It was time to move on.

Apparently it was at this time that the recriminations began and the hurt, anger and confusion started to surface. But to everyone's amazement the rest of Joy Division, who had been 'left behind', decided to continue, and within a short space of time they played a short instrumental set at the Beach Club, organised by Suzanne O'Hara. Subsequently they informed the world that from then on they would be known as New Order, which has as many possible meanings and connotations as you choose to give it.

There had been some speculation as to whether Ian would be replaced. Alan Hempsall of Crispy Ambulance, who had stood in for Ian when he was especially ill with his epilepsy, was a likely contender. Kevin Hewick, an eccentric and gifted solo artist, who had been featured on the *Factory Quartet* double LP, even auditioned for the part. He told me in 2006 that Martin was present, yet emotionally absent, at the audition, but was generous, kind and encouraging. The whole affair was desultory and Kevin sensed after attempting a couple of Joy Division's songs that no one had the heart or appetite for it. He continued, up until the present day, as primarily a solo artist and perceptive cultural commentator.

But New Order decided that they should go back into the studio, initially to record two songs left over from the JD repertoire – 'Ceremony' and 'In a Lonely Place'. They decided to return with Martin Hannett.

But if New Order felt it was also time to move on – and indeed christened their debut album *Movement* – Martin was trapped in a very different, lonely, place. For him it was to become stasis. The excitement and enthusiasm of the recording of *Unknown Pleasures* and to a lesser extent *Closer* was replaced with a weariness and emptiness and mounting sense of devastation. It was as if he knew his time had passed; the parade had moved on. He had begun to mistrust the machinations of Factory Records after the comparative success of *Unknown Pleasures* and harboured suspicions that he was being cheated out of his fair share of the profits. Of course his burgeoning heroin habit (eighty quid a gram in them there days) was voraciously eating away at any money that came his way.

The uneasy relationship between Tony and Martin was becoming more vexed. Martin had always been sceptical of Tony's more poppy taste in music, at times deriding him for his predilection for the more new wave outfits such as the commercial Blondie, with whom Tony was infatuated for a while, or mod-influenced The Jam. Martin could be highly critical and snobbish.

Then there was the matter of drugs that came between them. Martin had moved into darker and darker territory, whereas Tony had stayed on safer ground.

Martin had once told Tony, in regard to his drug of choice, heroin: 'The thing you have to remember about heroin if you are able to deal with it, is that it is the most wonderful thing in the world. Understand that; believe that and then maybe you can handle it.'

Tony never went near the stuff.

But Tony remained loyal to Martin, up to and beyond his death. These days he has little but praise for Martin's contribution to the success of Factory Records. That's not to say that he found being around Martin easy, especially in the later years of their uneasy partnership. It was Martin who persuaded Tony not to use a London plugger to promote JD's pop perfection 'Transmission', and as a result Tony ended up with boxloads of unsold copies. But it was Tony who tried to act as a go-between when Martin Hannett accused Martin Moscrop of ACR of being 'a fucking fascist' and almost refused to work with the group when they were working on ACR's *To Each . . .* in 1980. Later Tony would be supportive of Alan Erasmus's move to bring Martin back into the Factory fold in the late 1980s and introduced him to Shaun Ryder and the Happy Mondays clan and tried to help to restart his flagging, or nearly flagged, career.

Martin's sceptical mistrust of Tony and his cronies hardened into something much more venomous after Ian's death. Perhaps he blamed Tony in some way.

In this atmosphere, the recording sessions for 'Ceremony' and the album *Movement* were not happy ones. Peter Hook revealed that 'When we got to *Movement*, it was a real low point, for us and for Martin. He would sit at the desk and say "I'm not working until I get a gram of coke."'

Cocaine of course is the ultimate numbing drug. It numbs the mind, the emotions, the nose and the gums. The main effect of cocaine is to make you want more cocaine – so you can remain in your cool cocaine cocoon. Nothing can touch you. You become impervious and indeed imperious. It would become the designer drug of the 1980s – the Me Decade.

Peter Hook went on to observe: '[Martin] definitely began to lose it at that point . . . and we weren't much better . . . Martin would sod off to the little room at the back and say he wouldn't come out until he heard something he liked . . . I actually liked *Movement*, but I know why nobody else did . . . it was good for the first couple of minutes and then it dipped.'

And nobody else *did* seem to like it although it has moments, I believe, of startling beauty, melancholy and mordant melodicism. Even the sleeve is low-key, uninformative and understated. It was recorded in two weeks in the now hauntingly reminiscent Strawberry Studios. Everyone involved must have been painfully aware of the gap in their midst. There was no one for Martin to chat briefly to; there was no wonder boy to record late-night vocals.

Indeed the new group were still undecided as to what they would do about their vocal-less situation and almost by default Bernard Sumner took over – initially his voice sounding like a slight, light echo of Ian's booming baritone. The vocals were mixed way down and at times become nearly inaudible. The words too seem snatched, inconclusive and uncertain. There is never any sense of performance. Instead the musicians focused on the rhythms and textures and the album has an ambient feel to it.

Movement was released in November 1981. Its highest position on the albums chart was number 30, before it faded away. Bernard Sumner told *Melody Maker*: 'I absolutely hated *Movement*. I've hated it since I first heard it; never played it since. I was so angry having to put out a record that I didn't like.'

The writer Dave Thompson reckons that *Movement* is 'all mood and no magic'. Perhaps the alchemy had gone. There was no magician or magician's apprentice. There was little depth; all that remained was the surface sheen.

And yet a large number of recording artists try to achieve that clean ambience and those sinuous electronic rhythms – thus large parts of the electronica and drift movements: Aphex Twin, Autechre, Labradford, Tortoise, Heligoland, Mouse on Mars, Sabres of Paradise, LFO, My Bloody Valentine, Sigur Rós, to name but a few.

The record was panned by the music press, which had previously been enamoured with Joy Division's output. The *NME* reviewer tore into it claiming that 'it's terrifically dull' and *Sounds*, who were now championing the Positive Punk boys and the loutish Oi! brigade, dismissed it as 'utterly disastrous'. Martin, although he pretended otherwise, was hurt and stung by the reviews and the muttered comments of his contemporaries. He ventured out socially less and less. His production work became more pragmatic and a means to a (chemical) end.

A further 12-inch single was released on the Factory/Benelux imprint in December 1981. It was the end of another year, another era. It would represent the final collaboration between Martin and his erstwhile pupils. It comprised 'Everything's Gone Green', 'Mesh' and 'Cries and Whispers': cries and whispers indeed.

Peter Hook, never Martin's greatest admirer but always gracious nonetheless, remarked: '[Martin] taught us what to do very early on. We learnt the actual physics of recording from him . . . but in the end there was too much compromise from both sides.'

New Order would build on this tentative beginning with their next, self-produced, album *Power, Corruption and Lies*, which saw them break through commercially, especially with the massive global success of 'Blue Monday' and beyond. But Martin was to be left behind, as they moved on. Similarly A Certain Ratio, who were starting to enjoy some artistic acclaim and a cult following, had eagerly embraced the nu-dance sound, and chose not to work with Martin again. Even faithful Vini Reilly, after his first solo foray with *The Return of the Durutti Column*, never returned to ground Zero.

Was this the beginning of the end, the end of the beginning for Martin?

17

The relationship between Martine, my wife, and Martin was an intriguing one. I think he became fascinated to the point of obsession with her and on a number of occasions, after the baby was born, they went out scoring together, whilst I baby-nodded. Often they were gone for hours. One time they came back at 8 o'clock in the morning and mentioned that they had enjoyed a hearty cooked breakfast in a service station off the M6. Suzanne, who had a deep mistrust and dislike of the obvious trappings and vagaries of the hard drug lifestyle, seemed suspicious of their relationship – perhaps seeing it as a liaison dangereuse. In some ways Martine represented the prototype for Martin of the various doomed young women who would come after Suzanne and before Wendy 2.

I will never know what really transpired between them. I do know that the only time Martin ever injected heroin it was in Martine's company, and at her instigation. Martine told me about this whole episode one very smacked-out night; she recounted it to me as if it was a midnight movie that she had seen with a Joy Division soundtrack. Her recall and eye for detail were exceptional. I had no reason to doubt the veracity of her tale.

It's a damp, dank, dark, dirty evening.

Martin has left Cargo Studios where he has been working with Section 25 on tracks for their debut album, *Always Now*. Ian, who has been dead for nearly a year, used to champion the Blackpool boys to the extent of ending up in a fist fight whilst defending their reputation at a Factory Records New Year's Eve party. But he is no longer around to fight their corner. Section 25 is seen by many, perhaps unfairly, as a poor imitation of Joy Division: the songs without the singer, the sound without the feeling. And it sometimes feels like that to Martin, as if he is recording an empty shell, devoid of life or meaning: just the misery and monotony remain. He attempts to give it his best shot, to provide some shine and sheen. But the song titles alone give the morbid, moribund game away – 'Charnel Ground' and 'Haunted', a piece written in memory of Ian Curtis. At times he is beginning to feel as though he is already recycling the techniques that he utilised to such effect with Joy Division: the trebly bass high in the mix in 'Haunted', the heavily echoed vocals, the peripheral slightly distorted guitars. He has been employed, in his role as Factory Records in-house producer, to work with other bands, such as the Belgian combo the Names and the surreally monikered Crispy Ambulance. With the latter he has explored a different, brighter sound in an attempt to free himself of what is rapidly becoming a straitjacket trademark sound – the one he pioneered with Joy Division.

He is planning to take the master tapes down to Britannia Row in London to mix them, sprinkle them with some voodoo magic dust and turn them into something eerily special. Are you only as good as the material that you have to shape? Is there only so much that you can do with a limited palette? He relies on that chemical interaction with the musicians and particularly the singers, however tempestuous and volatile.

He is also faced with tensions within The Invisible Girls collective as they begin to think ahead to the third recording with John Cooper Clarke, after the comparative critical and commercial success of the second elpee, *Snap, Crackle and Bop*. That album will eventually become *Zip Style Method*, half of the tracks recorded in Martin's absence because CBS no longer trust him. By this time he has become renowned for going over time and budget in the studios, especially when the majors – CBS, EMI, Epic – are footing the bill. In his younger days he prided himself on being able to prise more money out of the financiers and to get away with biting the hand that fed him (and his habits). He has also grown used to the free-form democracy, at times seeming anarchy, that is Factory Records.

But he is becoming a bad investment, especially when stories have begun to leak out about his increasingly bizarre behaviour, in the studio, at the record label's expense. No one likes to have the piss taken out of them. The tale of him refusing to work until he had a gram of coke can't have helped his reputation. Nor his description of everyone else as being 'you're all a bunch of wankers'. Even the more narcotic bands like The Psychedelic Furs and The Only Ones have found him difficult if not impossible to deal with and word has got back to their paymasters.

So it is in this mood that he parks outside our house, in the middle of our street. By now, the house has a palpable air of menace hanging around it, like an unwanted visitor. He raps the knuckles of his right hand against the window pane: the secret knock. There is no twitching curtain. In fact there is no curtain, nor light. He peers into the darkened room. It looks empty. There seems to be broken glass on the floor. He knocks again. He needs to score. The session has overrun, the bloody bass player kept on screwing up. The bass part was blindingly easy, for Christ's sake. He was tempted to grab the instrument off the poor, po-faced kid and play the bloody riff himself – three notes, how difficult could that be?

He is irritable, starting to perspire, skin beginning to crawl. He hasn't had any decent gear for days. He has even resorted to doing some sulphate – never a good idea when you're withdrawing. He raps again. A figure appears in the darkened room. He feels that familiar flood of relief, almost elation; just the possibility of smack is enough to lift the spirits. It is Martine. She raises one hand in a pitiful attempt at a greeting.

She opens the door to him. Although it is chilly she is only wearing skintight black jeans and a skimpy sleeveless grey T-shirt. She is barefoot. She looks vulnerable and defenceless.

'Hiya Marti!'

She makes an attempt at levity. They call each other Marti: a sign of affection, familiarity and that bond that invisibly binds and blinds them.

'Where's Colin?'

'He's in Newcastle, visiting his sister.'

Martin can tell from the minimalist tone of her reply that she too is on the brink of withdrawal.

'How about the baby?'

'He's with Colin. In Newcastle. With his sister.'

Such is the extent of her exhaustion and lethargy. It reminds Martin of the group that he has just been working with: only capable of repeating a few, brief phrases.

Martin notices that both her arms are covered in dried blood.

'I'm trying to get a hit. I've only got a tiny bit of gear left. I spilled some.'

This is delivered flatly, but the tragedy is implicit.

'Let's go and score then. I've got plenty of cash. I'm flash!'

Martin tries to cheer her up, plays the older, jokey, daft brother.

'OK. Aye. Great. I've got to try and have this hit first though if you don't mind. I got a titchy bit that you can smoke if you like. Keep you going sort of thing.'

'Can I come in then?' he says with a feeble smile.

'What? Oh aye. Sorry.'

He follows her into the lightless house. They edge along the narrow corridor that is still in an unfinished stage of redecoration – the dark blue that I have become partial to suddenly stops halfway along a wall.

'He'll never finish that,' Martine remarks, as if reading Martin's thoughts. 'He writes songs about it instead.'

Martin follows Martine into the front bedroom. Little remains, apart from the beloved stereo system, the more cherished bits of vinyl, some clothes, including Babygros, strewn all over the floor. In amongst the items Martin notices several pairs of stockings – red, black, white, even baby pink. In the midst of these bits and bobs of woeful costuming and empty Peaudouce nappy boxes are her paraphernalia – the all too familiar needles, spoons and burnt matches and a semi-loaded works containing some vile-looking liquid – a potage of coagulating blood, cheap smack and baby powder, because that's what the bastards cut it with. Again Martin has to choke back the surge of sickly sadness that wells up inside him. Withdrawals, in the early stages, tend to make you feel overemotional. Moods can swing from remorse to regret to guilt to rage to loathing to euphoria to fury within the space of a minute. Somewhat like the effect of grief.

'Have that little bit. I was only keeping it back in case I had a dirty hit.'

The likelihood of that, given the contents of the syringe, seems extremely high, but such is the selfish need of the addict that Martin gratefully accepts the offer and quickly prepares to chase a tiny, harmless, much misunderstood, baby dragon.

As Martine searches for a vein, Martin heats the thin substance, definitely Rochdale Rough or Ashton Agony. It hardly manages to burn. The inner chemist wearily wonders why. He inhales what he can and there is a temporary lessening of the impending sense of doom and the creeping cramps.

'I can't fucking find one. I can't . . .'

She starts to slap at the insides of her thighs, she bashes her arms.

'Let's go and score. We'll try that friend of yours in Stalybridge. She's always got great gear.'

She spots one. Her concentration is total.

Martin holds his breath, which is fortunate considering he has just chased the final, meagre specks of badly tampered scag. She slips the jagged needle point into the tiny tot of a vein. She gently eases the plunger down the barrel and sends the discoloured consignment into her system.

Martin exhales slowly. Martine allows the dregs to infiltrate her bloodstream. There is a mild rush; she closes her eyes for a second to savour it. Martin allows himself to savour the image of her – the works hangs from her right wrist, still connected to her, metal in flesh; a few droplets of blood drip onto a bright yellow baby's sleeping suit, with a Donald Duck motif, which has been used to mop up the bleeding mess.

'Right then,' she announces cheerily. 'Let's go and see what our friend Kath has got tonight.'

And so, it is off to Kath's again. They both begin to feel the excitement and anxiety that the true addict experiences as they close in on the score. There is always the dreadful possibility that the dealer will be absent or won't have any junk. But there is also the fantasy that they will have just taken possession of a consignment of the cheapest, cleanest, strongest narcotic that has ever been refined: the elixir of the illegal drug world. Unconsciously addicts revert to a stage whisper as soon as they are in the proximity of their dealer. Perhaps they are worried that if they speak too loud it might frighten them away or draw the attention of 'the heat'.

Martin would prefer not to go into the houses of dealers, but he also has the addict's suspicious mind that tells him that if he hands over a wad of readies, even to Sweet Martine, a number of things will inevitably happen. Either Martine will pocket a handful of cash for herself for later, or the dealer will overcharge, or the two of them will connive and reach some petty criminal arrangement by which they both gain, but he is the loser, the sucker, the schmuck. And goddamn, no one wants to be a schmuck, no matter how large an advance from CBS or EMI or Factory Records they have in their real leather wallet.

She goes quickly, deftly, up the tiny path through the overgrown front garden with its abandoned, rusty child's bicycle and broken workman's hod. She glances over her right shoulder. Martin follows her, automatically keeping his head down. The secret knock on this window is elaborate and rhythmic. Martin imagines the jazz-funky bass line that could go on top of it. It could be a pretty good groove with a sprinkling of light pianoforte chords and some chunky rhythm guitar chops to add tone and flavour. He mentally stores it for the next Cooper Clarke sessions. Kath's pinched features appear so fleetingly that it could have been a hallucination or an awful apparition. She opens the green, peeling door just enough so that they can squeeze in past her into the dimly lit corridor.

'Oh, hiya,' Kath says in that instantly recognisable smackhead drooling drawl.

It signifies that she knows who he is, and that she knows he is more than likely well stacked, in the financial sense. Her pupils are microscopically small. She has the best moon tan of any junkie in north Manchester, which would suggest that, like a vampire, she has never seen direct sunlight. The phrase 'stick-insect-thin' was invented to describe her. She drags her grubby, bitten to the quick, blood-red nails down her lily-white cheeks. She does it so hard that you can hear the scratch, rather like an early rap number, something by Grandmaster Flash. Martin's hearing is so acute that it sometimes feels like he is living in Edgar Allan Poe's House of Usher. Her scratched cheeks are so drawn that they look hand-crafted. There are lines on her face that seem to have been borrowed from an Escher print. Her lips are a mere afterthought and barely conceal jagged teeth that have no idea of the existence of the dental profession.

'Well . . . you're in luck,' she whispers, overenunciating in that familiar manner. 'I've just gained possession' – she's going all technical and legalese on him now – 'of some very fine Iranian heroin.'

'Sounds good. How much?'

He wrong-foots her with his directness. He can see her doing mental arithmetic. He guesses that this will increase her annoyance with Martine: if she had known in advance that he was coming then she could have dreamed up an appropriate, overinflated price.

'Eighty?'

She shouldn't have suggested the question mark.

'For a gram.'

There is no implicit question mark in Martin's response. He knows that she is testing his knowledge.

'Oh yeah, aye, a gram, that's right . . . Do you want to try some?'

'Thank you, yes. That would be good.'

She pulls a bulging plastic bag full of scag out of her denim shorts pocket.

He takes a hit right there, using the paraphernalia protectively kept in an antique brown leather doctor's wallet, which he unearthed in an Irish shop whilst browsing around Dublin shops when he was there, at Windmill Lane Studios, recording '11 O'Clock Tick Tock' with U2 – their second single. To Martin's chagrin and annoyance they dumped him in favour of the ubiquitous Steve Lillywhite, and neither of the tracks that he recorded with them made it onto their debut album *Boy*. It is those slights and slurs that are beginning to hurt and harm him: death by a thousand cuts. 'Look out . . . here comes Martin Hannett.' 'Quick, hide . . . here comes Mad Marti.'

As soon as he starts to inhale the acrid smoke he knows that this is top-grade, numero uno, gear. It might even actually be Iranian heroin. It might actually not have been 'stepped' on. He ceases the chase half-way down the line. The warmth and the comfort are almost immediate. He holds it down as deep as he can: deeper than the deepest deep. The smoke circulates inside him. It finds its way into his bloodstream, his capillaries and his corpuscles. It coats his nerve ends with a secure blanket. It courses though his cranium and connects with the saucy synapses. It fills the fucking gap.

He experiences a sensation of complete emptiness, empty incompleteness. He struggles back from the edge. He wants to avoid the void; he doesn't want to kiss the abyss – not yet. He shakes his head, his curls fall into his face. He scratches at his neck – usually the non-intravenous drug user doesn't experience the constant itching of the needle junkie, but this gear is so damned strong and potent that waves of warmth are radiating up from his solar plexus and his lungs. He tries to force himself up out of the chair.

'I desperately need a holiday,' he thinks to himself.

He is in that twilight state where he is uncertain as to whether he is speaking his thoughts out loud or not. It is a state he will return to, with an awful vengeance, in the latter days of his alcoholic existence. It is a terrible place where the line between the inside and the outside has evaporated and more terrifyingly the outer seems to intrude on the inner. There is no longer any separation, no longer any defence from the hostile forces of the mundane and the banal.

He has begun to experience 'Martin Hannett' as someone else. Someone at one remove from the Martin who likes cornflakes for breakfast and hates the cold and likes pure wool. This is an odd position to be in; he needs to be careful. He must avoid believing his own press, be it gushing or appalling. He must be careful not to become his own myth. That way, surely, madness lies.

Back in the car, they decide to go back to Martin's. Suzanne is away, staying with Stephanie in London. His relationship with her is becoming ever more volatile. She has always been ambivalent about Martin's drug usage. She has a horror of drug dealers and the whole druggy, sordid, petty criminal milieu. It is always Martin who goes to score whilst she waits at the flat, fretting and shivering. Her attitude to Martine Helene and other more shady women on the periphery of Martin's life is suspicious. She can be protective and possessive. She worries that people are attracted to

Martin for the wrong reasons, for what he does, rather than who he is.

They drive the short distance to Martin's Didsbury flat. It is tucked away on a quiet cul-de-sac. It consists, as an estate agent will tell you, of the upper two floors of a Georgian town house. It has its own, discreet, entrance, at the side. The garden is well tended. There are flowers and bushes involved in some sort of botanical construct. Even the windows are cleaned regularly. There is nothing remotely rock 'n' roll or debauched about this location. That's the way Martin likes it. There is nothing like a bit of anonymity to keep you feeling comparatively safe.

Martin unlocks the four separate safety mechanisms; Martine follows him into the quiet tranquillity of the lower lobby. He repeats the locking ritual from the inside.

The flat is spacious, warm verging on sauna, shades of deep brown and orange – earthy colours. This is Suzanne's touch: the touch of the neurotic, erotic Earth Mother. Everything is orderly and neat. There is a small room immediately off to the left, which is Martin's office. It has a desk, telephone, stacks of tapes, Dictaphone, his recordings, ephemera, state-of-the-art audio equipment and headphones. On the wall is FAC 1 – the Peter Saville-designed poster for the very first Factory night at the Russell Club.

Across the corridor is the spare bedroom, currently unoccupied but previously inhabited by Stephanie (Formula) before she moved down to London to be with Dave. He is now recording with the recently revamped Ultravox – who have abandoned the creative experimentation of the John Foxx-era grouping, for something much more facile and commercial. They will soon hit pay dirt with their grandiose signature tune – the pompous and overblown 'Vienna'. They will never consider working with the volatile and erratic 'Mad Martin' Hannett. His place will be taken by the new breed of whizz-kid producers – Steve

Lillywhite, Martin Rushent, Mike Howlett, Mike Thorne and eventually the ultimate musical boffin – Trevor Horn.

Martin will be usurped in the favours of some of the bands that he has worked with, and arguably helped launch, by these young pretenders. The Furs will defect to Lillywhite; Orchestral Manoeuvres in the Dark will choose the safety of a Howlett production rather than a Hannett howl-round. U2 will opt for the experience and prestige of another green Eno world, despite their blueprint experience with Martin. Again it will be a decision based on pragmatism and that overriding desire for commercial success, which in their case will result in Global Domination.

Ever feel as though the parade has passed you by?

Then it's on either into the generously proportioned kitchen, which is always well stacked with smack snacks, nibbles, tasty morsels, wines, champagnes (for those cocaine soirées); or straight ahead into the sumptuous lounge, which is dominated by a black, studded three-piece suite and enormous Bang & Olufsen speakers. The floor is covered in ethnic rugs purchased from the hippy emporium On the 8th Day.

Further steps lead up to the inner sanctum of Martin's master bedroom.

Martine has only been here twice before, and both times were just passing, fleeting, dropping off gear, visits. She knows that I spent considerable amounts of time here. 'Do you want some coffee or juice or . . .'

Martin is an attentive host. You never offer alcohol to a friend when they're on the smack. It just isn't done.

'I'll make coffee,' Martin mumbles, suddenly self-conscious, insecure and uncharacteristically inarticulate. He is never that good around people. Machines and technology he is happy with. He is at his most secure when he is in control – in the studio or driving an automobile. He likes to be on the move. Music can create that sense of travel, the forward motion.

Martine takes a shower, checking the bathroom cupboards, just in case. You never know, there might be some Palfium or pethidine or even some delicious Diconal kicking about. But all they contain is peppermint mouthwash and some harmless Disprin. By the time she returns, Martin is sitting on the comfy settee. He has treated himself to another cheering trail of Stalybridge's finest. Two steaming coffee mugs wait patiently on the glass-topped table, which is handy for snorting cocaine on, because you can always see any white traces that you might have missed. He has arranged a display of biscuits on a china plate. Ginger nuts are surrounded by bourbons that are encircled by rich teas and garibaldis. Three packets of Marlboro are stacked on top of each other. He has a Lee Perry production on the turntable. Dub reggae is his preferred listening at the moment. It's all in the sonic details. Sometimes when he's in the studio with Chris Nagle, his favoured engineer, he sits at the end of the sound desk where all the effects are located. So he can play with the reverbs and delays and harmonisers. Perhaps unfairly, some of the musicians describe Chris as being babysitter to Martin's King Baby, but it's the combination of childlike experimentation and infantile adventure balanced by the pragmatic and practical approach that produces such exciting results.

The lights are way down low. Martin was one of the first to have a dimmer switch installed. He presciently once told Donald Johnson, the brilliant drummer from A Certain Ratio, that one day all musical reproduction equipment would be contained inside a little metal box – like a pod.

Martine enters the dimly lit room full of the swirling, swishing sounds of high-class Jamaican dub and the pungent, sinful scent of heated heroin.

'Your . . . gear . . . is there.' He indicates the japonais occasional table. 'And your coffee . . . and some biccies.'

It's really just a cosy evening in for the two of them.

A massively echoed rim shot reverberates around the room, travelling fluidly from speaker to speaker. Someone once genuinely mistook Martin's speakers for radiators. They have an unusual, aesthetically pleasing concave shape. It's all in the physics of sound, the sound of physics and indeed the physicality of sound. Some of Martin's productions have a physical effect on the listener. They are a visceral experience that affects the stomach, the solar plexus, the thorax as well as the ears.

Martine takes her little bag of tricks and kneels neatly on the faux-Peruvian rug. Martin leans forward, rests his elbows on his knees and then his clean-shaven chin in the palms of his hands. He is exquisitely, immaculately stoned.

The objects, the tools of the trade, are carefully laid out on the tray. There are household matches, tumbler of lukewarm water, silver needle, dessert spoon, gram of heroin, lemon squeezy and syringe.

She sets to work with the works. Her technique is deft, delicate. A lighter rhythmic dub track underscores her efforts. Her fingers dance. Her concentration is complete. Martin admires her fine focus; there is freedom in the concentration on a task. His father taught him that. People are often at their most attractive when they are focused on their work; in the world that they know and control. This is why guitarists can appear so sexy. It is also true of Martin himself. He comes alive behind a recording console.

Once the task is completed, she sits back on her haunches, loaded works in her right hand. She carefully squirts a tiny droplet out of the aperture of the needle, so as not to waste one single precious drop. It is sexier than foreplay. She keeps her eyes fixed on the tiny skin spot that is not covered with scar tissue. She removes the instrument from her mouth. She stalks her prey. She aims, then she spears. It's a perfect first hit. The sharpened steel punctures the vulnerable flesh. She pulls the plunger back. The blood explodes into the barrel, and then expands in slo-mo, before she presses it back to where it came from.

It's the slow, then suddenly fast effect that Martin has captured in some of his work with Joy Division that will later be picked up by the grunge guys like Nirvana and Pearl Jam. It's the sonic equivalent of a rush.

The hit is immediate.

'Oh fuuuuuck.'

Her head jerks back. The tendons on her neck strain. Her mouth opens wide and wild. She emits a gurgling sound from the back of her throat. Her whole body convulses. Martin instantly worries that she has inflicted a 'hot shot' on herself and that she'll 'go over'. He's picked up all the junkie terminologies, the Burroughs babble. He's a literate lad. He read Kerouac and Corso, Ginsberg and Ferlinghetti – the beat poets. Just as suddenly her head slumps forward, her mouth slack, needle still spearing her vein. She shudders again, less violently.

'Bloody hell, that's good gear.'

She cleans up swiftly. She replaces the articles on the tray, in exactly the same positions that they were in before she utilised them to such near-lethal effect. It is some weird game of chess: a mutant glass bead game.

'Can we listen to one of your records?' she lisps.

The lisp is not deliberate. It is a result of the power of the heroin. It is a side effect: a vocal side effect. Despite his opiate state he makes a mental note to try and achieve that effect in a forthcoming production.

'I'm not that keen on listening to stuff I've done. All I hear are the imperfections.'

'I won't hear them (sic) imperfections, Martin. I promise. I just listen to the songs.'

'All right then, if you insist.'

'Then maybe you'd like me to inject you.'

It sounds like the most obscenely intimate suggestion that anyone could ever make.

'I don't know . . .'

He has always been very queasy about needles, inoculations, blood samples.

'You could just try. Just once. Just the one time. One hit.'

She is seductive. She is the temptress, the Eve to his Adam. She is also challenging him.

'It won't hurt, not a bit. You can let go, Marti. You don't always have to be in control, you know. Sometimes it's fun to be washed away . . . I'll do it all, I'll tighten the belt, I'll get the vein up. I bet you got great veins, really easy. You'll like it so much. It feels so good: the rush. It's the best, it's even better than . . .'

She trails off modestly.

'What do you reckon Marti?'

She is more insistent with this than anything he has noted previously. This is her territory, her domain. This is the world that she inhabits.

He stands up, lights a cigarette. Martine is now sifting through his enormous record collection. She has found the 12-inch of 'Ceremony/In a Lonely Place' and is playing the 'Ceremony' side with its mournful, sweet melodious guitar line, underpinned by those Hannett-trademark depth-charge explosive snares and big bass drum. The guitars chime and rhyme, his homage to the summery sounds of the beloved Byrds.

'I love this one. It's got a great tune.'

'Not an entirely bad production either . . .' Martin is always the master of the self-deprecating remark. 'Not that the boys in the band necessarily agreed. Then again, what the hell do they know?'

'Is this all stuff what you've made?'

'Yep. I made all of that!'

He saunters over to her. He surveys his handiwork. Most of it is beautifully packaged within Saville's clean-lined designs. He feels proud of his creations.

'What about the one you did with Ian and them lot jus' before he did himself in?'

She searches amongst his oeuvre and finds *Closer* in its neo-classical, iconic packaging. The image of the mourners, bent, over the shrouded body has become the stuff of myth, legend and scholarship. Was it prescient and prophetic or just a twist of bad luck?

It's the record that he finds most difficult to listen to. Even the thought of it is rapidly followed by an onrush of unsavoury guilt and a dreadful foreboding.

'Why don't I hit you up first, then we can listen to it together and you can explain to me all the ins and outs and bits and bobs about recording and studios and trickery and all that?'

How can he resist? How can he say no? Martine straightens up. She has taken control. There is no confusion in her eyes, only purpose. 'Why don't you sit down? Take your jacket off.'

He rarely removes his clothes. 'You won't feel the benefit,' his mother would warn him. He likes to have many layers between him and the cold, hostile world. He likes pure wool, not synthetic fabrics. He takes off his denim jacket, folds it neatly, places it over the arm of the settee – just like in the doctor's surgery. He finishes his cigarette as she readies the medicine.

She takes his right hand in her left hand and extends his arm.

'Wow, you've got great veins. They're gorgeous.'

He feels proud of his great, gorgeous veins, in the way he felt proud at school of having 'strong legs, good for running'.

The rite becomes more primal, more Magick. She strokes her fingertips over his arm, as if entranced.

'I wish I had veins like these,' she mumbles through her mouthful of syringe.

Martin guesses that she is something of a connoisseur when it comes to veins and capillaries and corpuscles. He half expects her to ask him what blood group he is. He always wanted to be Rhesus Negative. (Great name for a band.)

'I can't believe I'm letting you do this to me.'

It is said more to break the tension than anything else.

'It won't hurt a little bit. I honestly promise.'

She rubs softly at her chosen target. Then she slaps it with three fingers. It is an electric sensation.

He cannot observe any longer. He leans his head back, rests his cranium on the warm leatherette.

'Oh that's a beauty . . . an absolute bloody beauty.'

Then just the slightest pin prick as she slides the tip of the needle into the pulsing, perfect vein; a moment as she draws the blood out through the dropper's neck and then she inches the plunger home.

He understands in that instant why it is referred to as a 'hit'. It slams into his chest, he grabs his neck and then he 'goes over'. He is convinced in that split second that she has killed him.

He gulps for breath like a drowning man surfacing in a freezing cold lake. Then he submerges again, he goes back under. Another surge of smack sweeps her away down her own private river. She mumbles and mutters to herself like a mourning widow or a death watch beetle. She grips Martin's shoulders tightly, hanging on to him for dear life. They float downstream together.

Martin emerges. He feels utterly cleansed and purified. His whole body is suffused with warmth and warm light. He is protected from all creatures great and small. He has been given unlimited access to the

Temple, into the Holy of Holies, the Inner Sanctum. He has received knowledge and wisdom. He will fear no evil, even if he walks and hangs out in the valley of death.

He has the ultimate backstage pass.

'That was very strong. Very, very strong. Maybe a touch too strong.'

Martine lifts her head from his chest.

'I thought you was dead.'

'So did I!'

'Let's listen to Joy Division then.'

Never was the band's name so apposite.

18

'The Railway Children are downstairs? How can that be? Is Hayley Mills with them?' Martin is incredulous.

It is 1981. There seems to have been a steady stream of young hopefuls, with increasingly ridiculous names, that have been sent to him so that he can hopefully 'sprinkle some of his magic'. They appear to be in awe of him or resentful that they don't have more input into the recording process or both.

'We would have some say in the mix, but he would have more.' (Vin, Section 25)

'Sometimes we were rather surprised by the results.' (The Names)

Some of them claim that he does very little and leaves most of it to the engineers – John Brierley or Chris Nagle.

The assistant engineer shrugs, trying to feign indifference.

'They say they've got an appointment with you. They say they're going to do some recording with you.'

'Do you know anything about this Steve?'

Steve Hopkins shakes his head slowly; he is concentrating on achieving exactly the right sound from the new keyboard that is in front of him. He is attempting to locate a setting that doesn't make it sound like a frog.

'Probably something that Tony has set up,' he suggests laconically.

'More than likely, Mikey,' Martin replies, even more laconically.

'They've come from Blackpool,' the assistant engineer offers.

'Well they'll have to go back to Blackpool,' Martin states bluntly.

'Are the illuminations on?' Steve enquires.

'I'll tell them,' the assistant says.

'Tell them to come up. Blackpool is a dreadful place,' Martin ameliorates.

The youthful assistant treks off dutifully.

'They all sing, well intone, as if they are Ian Curtis's idiot younger brother. They gaze at their shoes and shuffle about and want to die. That's not rock and roll, that's genocide.'

Steve recognises the Bowie quote and smiles tightly, his focus still on finding something remotely warm and human.

They are putting some extra backing tracks down for *Zip Style Method*, but it's proving time-consuming and the plan is to head off to Ridge Farm Studios and do the sessions. But Martin doesn't want to leave Manchester; he doesn't want to be too far away from his connections. Eventually it will go so over budget and schedules that Stephen Hopkins will be asked to finish it off in Martin's absence. He does so, unwillingly. Later, he will come to regret that decision and worry that it contributed to Martin's decline and crisis of confidence, because underneath what could be a brash and surly exterior, Martin suffered from insecurity and self-doubt like most artistic individuals. You don't become a drug addict, alcoholic, overeater if you feel great about yourself and endlessly confident of your achievements. Martin is a perfectionist. He remembers the one thing, out of a hundred done right, that he feels he has done wrong. At times he can barely listen to his own work because all he hears is the imperfections. He would willingly mix a track endlessly if someone would be willing to pay the bill.

The Railway Children troop into the studio. They all look identical. They are all wearing shades of grey, long coats, hair obscuring their eyes.

'So . . . you wanna be rock and roll stars?'

They look at their shoes. They don't get the Byrds reference. They don't get it.

'Do your mums know where you are?'

Martin chortles. They shuffle slightly in unison.

'We'll have to replace you all first.'

Steve looks up. There is a manic glint in Martin's eyes.

The Railway Children realise that they are in the presence of greatness and possibly madness, so carry on gazing at their scruffy shoes.

'We will have to replace you with Real Musicians.'

They sneak glances at each other. Is he serious?

Martin chuckles and grins wickedly to himself. Steve shakes his head enigmatically.

Is Martin serious?

19

The disappointments were beginning to take their toll on Martin. His musical adventures beyond Factory's wheels of steel included contracts as hired sonic gun for The Only Ones, but personality and egos clashed with Only One Peter Perrett, who apparently accused Martin of being unreliable – surely a classic case of the kettle calling the pot black. Peter was well known for his myriad dalliances and open relationships, and the combined vast drug intake and general mayhem resulted in only three tracks before the group decided to use the more reliable Colin Thurston instead. Similarly U2, who seemingly had been disappointed with the results of the Hannett Dublin sessions and were nonplussed by his mind games and haughty demeanour (it's always hard when you meet one of your godlike heroes and find out that they have feet of clay). Even The Psychedelic Furs described his sound for them as 'too murky' and also opted for a Lillywhite production rather than a Murkydark one. With A Certain Ratio and The Durutti Column also leaving him, he was (very) high and dry.

But a few offers continued to come his and Steve Hopkins's way.

So it is that they find themselves in the prestigious Britannia Row Studios in London. It reminds Martin of the *Closer* sessions: the associations are not exactly positive. He has already detected 'ghosts in the machines'. They are going to do some demos with Paul Jones. Paul was the original lead singer with Manfred Mann, before going solo, and playing the lead part in the iconoclastic film *Privilege*, the story of a rock messiah martyr. He had a bit of a hit with the title song 'Privilege (Set Me Free)', later to be covered to devastating effect by Patti Smith, the High Priestess of Punk, on her *Easter* album. She mixed the song lyrics (by Jones and a young Mike Leander) with Psalm 23 and the line 'Oh I'm so young, I'm so god damn young'.

Paul has of late started turning his talents back to more earthy authentic blues fare but with diminishing returns. So his record company and his management agency have decided to put him in the studio with a more contemporary producer and hopefully give him something of a new wave sheen and futurist shine.

If these sessions work out well there is talk of work with other ex-sixties pop stars. Names such as Dusty Springfield (the best white female voice in pop), Scott Walker (of the wonderful Walker Brothers), Sandie Shaw (of barefoot fame and silly name), Peter Noone (originally a Manchester boy, Herman from Herman and the Hermits), Davey Jones (lead singer of the Monkees and another Manc lad) have all been mentioned.

Martin and Steve have joked about doing a doom-filled version of Herman's 'No Milk Today', in which 'milk' becomes a symbol for everything good, organic and eternal, or a punked-up, Ramonesesque 'I'm a Believer' from the Monkees' back catalogue. It could all be lucrative as well as a laugh. They have even pencilled in doing a cover of a cover with Paul Jones revisiting 'Privilege' as seen through Patti Smith's eyes and really going for a full-on gothic treatment of Psalm 23 with Bach fugue overtones and wheeling in a 23-piece (it would have to be 23) orchestra.

'Surely goodness and mercy shall follow me all the days of my life and I shall dwell in the House of the Lord for ever, god damn, god damn, god damn . . .'

'Loads of reverbed cellos, delayed violas, echoed piccolos,' Martin enthused in his excitement. Then they have toyed with a funked-up 'Do Wah Diddy Diddy', with extra wah-wah from the Manfreds' songbook, and a note-perfect paean to the pop perfection of 'Pretty Flamingo'. Martin hasn't seemed so positive and creative since the early JCC sessions of *Disguise in Love*.

But as soon as they hit outer London, Stephen driving the anonymous hired Hertz car that the record company has provided for them (Martin has dismissed it as 'soulless'), a cloud has descended around Martin's head. Steve can almost see it out of the corner of his eye – a rain-filled, grey-tinged cumulus or more likely a nasty nimbus.

They have been booked into adjoining rooms in the Hilton Hotel, which Martin has also derided as 'a glorified car park'. Martin has reappeared from his hotel suite looking a little more human and a little less hateful, having done a few lines of heroin, but then they hit Britannia Row Studios and the ghosts swirl around and hide themselves in the gathering storm clouds and Martin picks up 'lousy, fucked-up, fatal vibrations'.

He takes a cursory glance at the list of suggested session musicians and condemns them as 'has-beens, hacks and jazz-funk rockers'.

The first rhythm section is due in thirty minutes. Steve is trying to organise the rather cramped studio so they can achieve a live feel and maybe just jam together for a while to get the size of each other. Martin is wandering around looking exactly like a bear with a sore head, kicking the console, complaining about the foldback, dissing the equipment.

'I'm going back to Manchester, back to rainy Manchester. It's too dry down here. I need my own equipment. This is a bunch of shiny shit.'

Steve knows the real reason. He wants to be near his dealers. 'Martin, they're due in half an hour. These are all good players.'

'Players? Players!' Martin pounces on the word and makes it sound obscene.

Steve tries to contain his annoyance and dismay.

'Martin, if we blow this one . . . What shall I do with them?'

'Play with them then, play with the players. Jam! Jam around "Johnny B. Goode" for five hours. Do an extended version of "My Way". How the fuck should I know?'

Martin stands in the doorway. His fists are clenched, his nails pressed deep into his palms in self-harm. He knows he is destroying his career; he knows that he is destroying his Self. There are tears in his eyes – tears of frustration, fear, self-loathing and deep disappointment.

'Martin . . . please . . . don't . . .'

Steve's plea is gracious, generous, understanding and totally forgiving. But Martin turns his back.

Martin walks away.

20

By 1986 Martin was at the beginning of a long-drawn-out, bitter and acrimonious financial feud between him and the rest of the 'directors' of Factory Records. What once had been an ideological dream of a freewheeling independent record label had dissolved into tiffs and tantrums. Claims and counter-claims, rather than counter-culture. It was the building of the Haçienda Club that really caused a rift.

'This isn't Renaissance Florence, this is Dark Ages Manchester,' Martin had told Tony as they looked around the building site that would become the Haçienda.

Wilson had ignored him. Martin never liked being ignored. He had a temper.

'Is this real?' Martin continued through clenched teeth. 'Are we really doing this? You've actually gone and built it. How much?'

'Seven hundred thousand quid,' mumbled a stoned, pragmatic Rob Gretton.

'Now I know where my music budget has gone,' riposted Martin. 'You realise that we've got nothing in common. I'm a genius. You're all wankers. You'll never see me again. You don't deserve to see me again.'

The Haçienda, affectionately known as the Hac by the regulars, was first and last and always a nightclub, a glorified discotheque, a post-industrial Palais de Dance. It was all chrome and bright lights and shiny surface, and arguably just surface shine. It became spiritual home to the Manchester brand of rave, trance and later trip hop. It was host to live music, but it was foremost a deejay's and whizzed-up dancer's stomping ground, as the deejays became the superstars of their era.

Tony had become tied to the Haçienda, which he claims only ever lost him money. Rob Gretton was by now managing a world-class, internationally successful band in New Order. Saville was long gone, but would pop up to see how they were all faring and what the

Haçienda looked like – in some ways it was a pastiche of his designs for living.

The rest of Britain had also become infatuated with rave and its poppier, idiot cousins like Handbag and Happy, whilst in America, grunge had emerged from Seattle and the British rock fans took to Nirvana, Pearl Jam, Sonic Youth, Mudhoney and Stone Temple Pilots, all of whom acknowledged a debt to the Martin Hannett-produced sound of Joy Division. They played fast-then-slow and loud-then-quiet. Britain had its own grunge-inflected rock bands in the shape of The Cult, The Mission and The Almighty. The Cure and Siouxsie and the Banshees had amazingly survived and become hugely successful, whilst retaining their integrity and individuality. At times The Cure's songs sounded exactly like New Order numbers and vice versa. World music was becoming a buzzword, chill-out was just round the corner. And of course rap and hip hop grabbed the attention of urban youth. Style seemed to be winning the battle over content. The age of the live and gigging band, slowly building up a following before recording that crucial first album, seemed to be over. This became the age of the compact cassette, the Walkman. Music was less of a social thing, more of a personal quick match-and-mix fix. The edge and darkness and danger of music like JD's, although still echoing, seemed to have been lost as production techniques became ever more clinical and cynical, ever more linked to computer technology, and the equipment took over. Eventually, anyone could be made to sound good with digital equalisers and push-button chorus effects and one-click digital delays. Anyone could make music on their home computer.

Martin detested the Haçienda Club and saw it as an intrinsic part of his nemesis. 'Who wants to run a fucking nightclub?' he once yelled at a bunch of musicians who were interested in working with him. He had sent a lawsuit to Tony in New York, by fax, in an attempt to stop the Haçienda opening. He was on one-fifth of Factory Records' profits, but he believed they were swindling him. 'I'll never understand why he couldn't accept that arrangement,' Tony Wilson later commented.

And Martin's use of drugs was not helping his state of mind.

The last time Martin sees Martine, it is as though they are in a hundred bad and brilliant movies. It is *cinéma-vérité*, kitchen sink drama, tawdry tragedy, tragicomedy, gloomy farce. He is withdrawing badly. His eyes are rheumy and runny. He is snivelling. He is cold despite the old green cardy. She is huddled by a small window, by a wall; guns have shot over her head. There is a bare mattress with an institutional grey blanket on the floor. Three cigarette stubs have been put out on the black floorboards, even the carpeting has been torn apart. The baby is with her father, and I have fled from Manchester. She has been left in the house with three dangerous drug dealers.

Martin feels that queasy, uneasy, beastly feeling in his guts again. He hack-coughs, there is a sharp pain in his lungs. He feels sick. Maybe one of Martine's friends will give him some junk on tick. He hates to ask though. He has his pride. He's a nearly famous record producer; he's a magician in the studio. He shouldn't have to beg, borrow or steal.

Both of them are sorely in need of a fix as they set out into the night.

'You haven't got any cash have you.'

It is a bold statement. She knows they would have been gone long before if he had.

'Cash flow problems, I'm waiting for an advance, fucking record companies and their minions. I'm not going to start selling my . . .'

He stops himself short. He doesn't want to tempt fate, for he suspects that fate has got it in for him, is holding some kind of personal, supernatural grudge. Some mix-up at the bank.

'You got your car?'

He nods curtly, knowing that selling his precious Volvo might have to be a consideration one day. That and his sky-blue Stratocaster. In the end you sell your soul.

'We'll stop off at the garage.' The garage is Ted's Garage. It's an old-fashioned garage on the dual carriageway. It is an old-fashioned garage with a dual purpose – men come here both for petrol and for women. There is a discreet parking lot at the side of the forecourt. A few cars are hiding there surreptitiously.

'I shan't be too long,' she assures him. He watches her clack across the forecourt in the slip-on, strappy, fuck-me high heels.

He feels let down and abandoned. Each rejection hurts. He knows that he's getting a 'reputation'. They are beginning to see him as a liability. Steve and John finished the last tracks of *Zip Style Method* in his absence, behind his back, before sheepishly bringing the master tapes round to his flat hoping for his approval and benign blessing. Well, they didn't get it. The tracks were weedy and spineless. They were piss poor pastiches of his work. And he's hearing that more and more in the productions of his competitors. They are taking his trademark drum sounds and putting them behind dumb disco divas and meaningless chugging, choppy guitars.

It was fun when it all began in Cargo and Strawberry and Alan's flat on Palatine Road and Peter's lofty ideas and ideals for living and Wilson's machiavellian scheming and proselytising and the poppy Situationist sloganeering. Now half of the buggers won't talk to him and the other half treat him like a mad genius – a rocking Rasputin or Vlad the Producer.

He looks at his watch. Usually this gives him a degree of pleasure: it is a very expensive Rolex with all kinds of fascinating features and little twiddly bits, but on this occasion it gives him none. Only fifteen minutes have passed since Martine mounted the steps at the back of the garage. He finds himself wondering how much he could get for the timepiece from a pawnbroker. It's the slippery slope. First it's your watch, then your car, then your sky-blue Strat guitar. Nothing is sacred. Everything has its price. The only thing that he wants in this God-or-money world is some smack. That is the deal; that is the equation.

He sees Martine approaching across the forecourt.

He immediately knows that she is junked up. She is OK. It infuriates him. He experiences a rush of righteous rage.

'How long have you been gone?'

He's aware of the feebleness of the line.

'Not that long. I got you some gear.' He takes the sweaty wrap from her. The smack is wrapped in newspaper, a torn fragment of the *News of the World*. The print has mixed with the powder. There is less than a ten-quid deal left. He knows that she has done in (sic) the rest of it, in the cubicle, in Ted's sauna, in betrayal.

His anger suddenly subsides. All that he feels is emptiness, impotence, exhaustion and vast disappointment. He digs a thumbnail, it doesn't matter which, into the pathetic package. Who wants yesterday's papers; who wants yesterday's girl?

He blocks one nostril. He snorts the infected grains up the other nostril. It has been badly stepped on. Probably less than 25% heroin remaining. The rest could be baby powder, Vim, cooking salt, gravel or gravy granules. It takes but the merest edge off his horrors.

He clenches his jaw. Martine is stoned enough to be oblivious to his murderous mood: any bugger else could see the dark clouds gathering and hanging over him. He accelerates down the dual carriageway. He tempts fate, but fate sniggers and takes the piss.

They are rapidly approaching the crossroads.

'Martin. I don't want to go back there.'

She says this totally flatly and sincerely.

Martin chokes back the taste of guilt, remorse, anger, hurt, betrayal.

'Get a bus then.'

She bites her knuckle.

'It's OK. I can handle those fucking miserable bastards. I'll throw the fuckers out into the street. I'll call the squad down on them. I'll chop their heads off. I'll knife them in their sleep. I'll kill all of them.'

She snarls this tirade of violent fantasy. Martin believes that she is entirely capable of a minor genocide (sic).

He drops her off anyway. She gets out of the car. She walks and doesn't look back. He drives away.

They never see each other again, alive.

21

It is now 1991. Martin recorded very little between 1982 and 1988. He worked with a youthful Stone Roses, but the band were not happy with the results and singer Ian Brown commented to the rock journalist Nick Kent: ‘It was a disaster. He was only half there.’

On a personal level also, things are messy. After the collapse of his long-term involvement with Suzanne it would seem that Martin had a succession of brief dalliances with women who were younger and more impressionable than him. Perhaps these were ‘producer’s groupies’ who were attracted to the myth as much as the man. These were almost silent goth girls with pallid complexions and dark clothes and enigmatic expressions. There was one in particular who appeared at his side a lot, a Sister of Mercy maybe, but no one is quite sure of her name.

In the mid-1980s, in his wilderness years, Martin met and eventually married Wendy 2. Martin’s family was concerned, worried that she could be a drain on his dwindling financial and emotional resources. After Martin’s death they helped her out with a monthly allowance and by paying some bills.

The last time he was in the Haçienda it was for a video shoot for a track that he had recorded. The incident is usually credited to a shoot with the Happy Mondays, and even Martin in his addled state afterwards was unclear who the hell he was with or what for. In fact it was a video shoot for a lesser-known Madchester band, New Fast Automatic Daffodils. It was part of a promotional package to promote an EP of new bands featured on a compilation that Martin had contributed to. Not unlike *A Factory Sample*, years previously.

Whoever it is they have a shopping trolley. As soon as he sees it he starts to tremble in terror.

He is overweight – near 20 stone, shabbily clothed, face bloated and slack, curls of oily hair falling across his bloated visage. He seems to have difficulty maintaining any sort of balance, never mind equilibrium.

'Martin, would you mind getting in the trolley so we can push you about?' a tall lad with curly hair and a wispy beard asks him as pleasantly as he can.

He has lost the power of speech. He tries to shake his head, but he nods it instead, it is less effort.

'Good lad,' says some other johnny-come-lately.

He stands stock still staring at the metallic object. He starts to cry. They think he is laughing. They all begin to chuckle and chortle, imagining that they are sharing the joke.

Two of them try to lift him in. No good. Four of them have a go. He is still trying to shake his head but it keeps on nodding instead. An arm and a leg each, they heave and hoist, they huff and puff and lift him up and then somehow cram him into the trolley so that he can't budge and they cheer and the track begins to blast out of the Haçienda's shit PA system. It is dancey, rhythmic, he can't remember producing it. They start to wheel him around the deserted club, faster and faster.

They clap their clappy hands and stomp their stompy feet and blow their whistles and wave their arms and chubby girls with painted faces crowd around him and leer and jiggle their bouncy breasts in his face.

He can't breathe. He feels he will asphyxiate. He starts to vomit with vertigo and panic. He has to swallow back his own sick and bile. His head is lolling from side to side. This is it: the moment that he has foreseen and feared for so long. His head is going to come off his neck and roll around the shiny dance floor and they will kick it about and score a goal with it and the crowd will rise to its feet and roar approval and it will look really good on the video and everyone will wonder how the hell they did it and whatever happened to Martin Zero Hannett?

But in 1988 he managed to cook up some of the old magic for the

Happy Mondays, including their breakthrough single 'Wrote for Luck' and the *Madchester Rave On* EP, which curiously became one of his few chart hits, after earlier commercial success with Jilted John. Certainly, some of his old spirit remained when he saw Tony Wilson for the last time: Tony greeted Martin with an affectionate 'Hello Hannett, you wanker', perhaps referring back to the Haçienda contretemps.

Martin swung on his swivel chair in characteristic manner, pulled his hand out from under his bottle-green jumper and pretended to have a gun.

'Now then Martin, you're a big lad, but you're out of condition and you can't hurt me,' Tony admonished.

'Well then why don't you fuck off and let the Men finish their work,' Martin replied with his best evil leer.

That, seemingly, was the last time that Those Two ever saw each other.

He hired out his skills, however blunted by then, to newcomers such as the World of Twist, Kitchens of Distinction and Andy Couzens's (formerly of The Stone Roses) new band, The High. He had helped create a beautiful replica of the Rolling Stones' 'She's a Rainbow' with the World of Twist, that masterfully combined 60s psychedelia with 90s dance and heralded the Madchester sound, and its crazy brother baggy, which eventually lurched into the whole 90s Britpop scene heralded by yet another Manc band of bad lads – Oasis – and their rivals, Blur and Pulp.

Martin was talking about promoting some of those groups, so eventually Mick Middles managed to get through to him and arranged to meet him outside his small office near the Celebrity Bar close to Granada Television Studios.

On reflection it might have been an unwise choice.

Mick waits outside the green building where the office is located for nearly an hour in the Mancunian mizzle. He sees Martin, and an unnamed accomplice, emerge staggering from the Celebrity Bar.

They could well have been ejected by a doorman. Mick is far too gracious to ask. He is shocked by the size of Martin. He hasn't seen him for a few years. He must weigh in at at least twenty-two stone. He is holding on to his companion's shoulder like a blind man. But it is the blind leading the blind. They are staggering so much that they are literally weaving from one side of the road to the other and passing celebrity motorists are sounding their horns and yelling superstar swear words out of their Mercedes at him. Martin seems entirely oblivious to the chaos that he has created. His assistant is thin and weaselly and probably only in his late twenties.

Martin stops in the middle of the road, raises his massive head up to the heavens, breathes in the fumes.

'Smell that Manchester air!' he exhorts in a voice that seems to have dropped an octave and has become more cracked croak and wizened wheeze than vocal.

'Mick, my man, lovely to see you: I am so sorry if we have kept you waiting at all, at all. We've been bummed!' He overenunciates every syllable in his courageous attempt at communication. It is as though he is reinventing the English language as he speaks, or attempting to recall it. It is reminiscent of the final track on David Bowie's *Low*, 'Subterraneans', because there are words that we recognise but they have lost sense and syntax. They are being reconfigured into a private, encoded, language. This will be the semantic route that Martin descends in the final years, ultimately followed only by his faithful translator David Rowbotham. It is often the last sanctuary for the chronic alcoholic, the terminal drug addict and the insane.

'That's OK,' Mick concedes decently.

'Lead on Macduff!' Martin bellows, then he splutters, then attempts to light a cigarette (an Embassy Regal; the days of Marlboro have passed), and then almost collapses against his accomplice, who is never introduced.

The co-conspirator leads them into the tiny office. There are only two chairs.

Martin waves Mick into the swivel seat behind the desk, which is covered in sweetie wrappers, flyers, empty bottles of cough medicine and final demands. Mick is reminded of his meeting with the man many years before in the creative environs of Music Force. The Force has long deserted him. The nameless one unfolds into the battered old chair. Martin unceremoniously collapses onto the threadbare puce carpet. His crony curls up in the chair, hugging his knees to his chest as if he has recently been attacked. Mick notices there is blood dribbling from Martin's lower lip. His left eye looks as though it is recovering from a recent punching. It seems as if he has slept in his colourless clothes for several lost weekends and weeks. There is a yachting magazine tucked into his stained raincoat pocket.

'Down to business then, eh Mick?'

Martin tries to sit cross-legged, but can't get one knee over the other.

'We're putting together a new label, forget Factory. All this Madchester stuff, there is, are, is, what should it be? Never mind the bollocks, here is . . . anyway a lot of fairly decent bands to be honest, Frank. Or to be frank honest, to look at it another way, as it were, was . . . Was Not Was, that sort of stuff, mutant disco, dirty dancey shite. You know the kind of thing. So we reckoned we might launch it with a festival. But we need a bit of sponsorship, do you know what I mean, Mike? These things seldom, if ever, pay for themselves, frankly.'

'Which bands? I might have heard of them.'

'Oh yeah, you'll have heard of them, Mitch. You will have heard them. If you haven't done as yet, then you certainly soon so will: you and every other bastard. No offence meant, Mickey, I didn't mean to suggest that you're a bastard, far from it. You always seemed like a decent kind of fella when you were with the . . . that . . . those . . .'

He begins to keel forward; catches himself just in time.

'We are talking – The Blue Mondays, the Happy Chappies, the World of Fix, the New Slow Jesus and Daisy Chain: all brilliant, Malcolm. They just need polishing up a bit and some decent exposure. But it's money that I'm after Michael. That's what I want.'

He says this in a childlike manner, his face creasing and breaking and tears filling his eyes.

Then he falls forward flat on his face.

22

Most of the people who saw Martin in the last few weeks of his life remember meeting him in a pub. They claim that he had been banned from a number of establishments. His house was up for sale. He was flat broke. Some of them believe that he had started using narcotics again, after a period of abstinence and/or had a methadone prescription. Some of them recall him calling round at their houses at ungodly hours with bizarre requests. Some of them even believe they saw him staggering around the streets of Chorlton on the last night of his life.

So the lonely death of Martin Hannett was recounted to me by a number of different sources.

It is the evening of 17 April 1991. Martin has decided that he needs to take what remains of their sitting room furniture upstairs, as the house is likely to be repossessed very soon and prior to the repossession the bailiffs are expected to come round and rob all the frigging furniture. He and Wendy 2 moved to a cheap terraced house in run-down Chorley a few years ago. It has been FOR SALE for seven months but the only prospective buyer refused to come in beyond the front door when they got a whiff of the state and stench within. The writing, quite literally, is on the walls. He has painted, in bold black brush strokes, 'DAMNED HOUSE, HOUSE OF THE DAMNED', at strategic points all over the fading yellow walls. There is only a hideous mauve three-piece suite and a hefty bookcase stuffed with old but precious tomes, yachting magazines, litigations, court orders, bibles, summonses, fines, *Helicopter Monthly*, old contracts and a very few of his records. His Records – the ones that he recorded. Most of them he has sold to collectors and vultures.

Although he doesn't know it, not far away, Martine is doing a two-year stretch in Styal Women's Jail for handling stolen goods. I am in

Newcastle upon Tyne, working in a travelling theatre company, with a prescription to keep me away from street drugs and danger and the seeds of a possible recovery growing somewhere inside.

Because Martin is now so obese – twenty-two stone and counting – there is an enormous strain on his already beleaguered, poor old lovelorn heart.

He decides it's probably best to pay a quick visit to the pub before he starts serious furniture shifting. The public house is one of the few places these days where he is in human company.

It will have to be the real-deal, down-at-heel, spit-and-sawdust hostelry a few blocks away as he's been barred from the three more homely taverns that are nearer. He has picked up the weekly methadone script that morning. He limits himself to two 25 milligrams.

Martin picks his crumpled raincoat off the floor. He more or less lives downstairs these days. Wendy has kicked him out of the bedroom for being too messy and noisy. She's tried kicking him out of the house a few times too; one time he escaped to his sister Julie's but they kicked him right back. He couldn't blame them. He has become a frigging liability. He knows that.

There is a battered old lilac Dansette in the corner but he seldom has the heart or the inclination to listen to music. It depresses and aggravates him. Anyway, down here he is closer to the kitchen and the downstairs toilet – if he needs to eat, piss or be sick.

He rummages around in the pocket of his grey raincoat – once it was chic and smart and knowingly post-industrial – a gift from some-one nearly famous. He finds the cheque for £9.08 from U2's publishing company. It arrived this morning along with the final final demands. Once he received royalty cheques for thousands of pounds, then that became hundreds and now it is down to this – £9.08. There is a guy in the pub – Chris or John or Terry – who might give him a fiver for it. He has no means of cashing cheques himself any longer.

He is uncertain what season it is. But it's drizzling. He wraps the coat around himself.

'An old raincoat won't ever let you down,' he mumbles to himself.

He can't recall one shred of the melody. It was Rod the Mod who covered the song, a good gutsy cover version. Now he's poncing around America kicking footballs around stadia, shagging blonde Swedish nymphets. It's all right for some. The Faces, they were a good pub band. Nothing more or less, they knew their limitations.

He almost goes into The Swan before remembering he's barred from that one too: an unfortunate altercation with the landlord. He's hungry. He is always hungry. There is never enough food in the house. Often there is no food in the house. He passes the flat where those kids who work the security at the fucking Haçienda live. If those prats at Factory had invested in a proper studio and some classy equipment instead of squandering it all on some tawdry dance piss palace then he wouldn't be in the bloody state that he finds himself in now.

Sometimes he drops in for a visit in the wee small hours just as they're getting back from their night shifts and they give him some frozen peas or a pork pie and he regales them with fragmented tales of Factory Records shenanigans and they try and comfort him by assuring him that the Haçienda is full of arse-licking wankers and wannabes and that the music and the drugs are shit. Sometimes they have garish chicks with them and as he stumbles off he hears them ask the lads 'Who the fuck is he?' The boys whisper in hushed tones, 'That is Martin Zero Hannett,' and they shake their heads and repeat, 'Who the fuck is he?'

He arrives outside The Shit and Bucket or The Spit and Fuckit or whatever the hell it is called. His short-term memory is so splintered these days that he loses entire chunks of his low-grade life. It sometimes feels as though he is constantly coming round to consciousness with a jarring jolt and no recollection of how he ended up in the alleyway covered in urine or lying in an overgrown garden with thistles in his face.

There are only a few desultory loners and losers in the Spartan bar. It is a public bar that has been reduced to the absolute basics. There is the bar itself, which doesn't serve crisps or peanuts. The plastic furniture is nailed to the floor. There is sawdust on the floor. You can see through to the Gents urinals. You can take bets on how fast lager turns to piss. Nobody knows where the Ladies toilet is and nobody can remember what Ladies are.

Everyone refers to the barman as 'barman'. There might be two, but if there are they are pretty interchangeable. Someone once claimed that they were called Paul and Barry and that in a previous life they had been the sixties singing sensation the Ryan Brothers, but this has remained entirely unsubstantiated.

Fortunately Martin's nefarious contact Chris or Dave or John is sitting near the door, his favoured spot, just in case he needs to make a sudden exit.

'Yalritemarti?' he mumbles, managing to half raise a right hand.

Martin leans against the Formica-topped round table – no square edges in here. He is panting heavily, out of breath, out of time, out of sorts, but for the moment maybe wrote for luck. 'I have a cheque from the bank of U2, you know who. The Irish stadium mega super . . .'

He fishes it out of his raincoat pocket. Chris or Pete or Steve takes a monocle from the top pocket of his shabby threadbare royal blue blazer. He spreads the cheque out on the table top next to his pint of stout.

'It's the genuine article Martin. It's the real McCoy.'

'I should hope so.'

'You don't see many of these about nowadays.'

'No, I don't. They should have done their first album with me.' It is a rare moment of clarity and lucidity. 'We would have created something otherworldly together. He was a good kid that Bongo.'

'Bono,' Alan corrects, but Martin's mind has gone.

For a moment he is back in the secure confines of a steel and chrome studio with the obscenely gorgeous ARP Omni-2 synthesiser and a pornographically pretty Powertran Transcendent 2000 and a halfway decent tenor singer with some halfway decent lyrics and the semblance of a melody.

'I'll give you a tenner for it,' Tommy offers, echoing the tenor in Martin's mind. 'But first allow me to purchase you a beverage of some alcoholic origin.'

''Kinnel Tommy, thank you kindly,' Martin enunciates.

'The pleasure is exclusively mine,' Tommy ripostes.

He is in a generous mood. Not only that though, he feels as though it's a special occasion, as if the once mighty Martin might be moving on.

'Are you moving on Marti?'

'We're meant to be moving, correct. Tomorrow . . . and tomorrow . . . creeps on this petty pace from day to day . . . and all our yesterdays are . . . all our yesterdays . . .'

It is gone: a blank.

'All our troubles seemed so far away, eh Mart?'

Martin slumps onto the plastic scoop-shaped seat. Only one cheek of his arse is lodged. He wobbles precariously.

'Help yourself to a fag, Marto,' Tommy proffers as he negotiates his way to the bar and the barman.

'Thanks Tommy, God bless you Tommy,' Martin mutters.

His psyche slips out of gear, as it too frequently tends to nowadays. 'Everybody's happy nowadays'. What remains of his active brain cells makes the synaptic connection. Buzzcocks, blessed Buzzcocks, who were so much a part of the start of his journey. Before it all turned to boredom, boredom.

'Howard and Pete should have stayed together,' Martin speaks his thoughts out loud. The distinction between the interior monologue and the exterior dialogue has become blurred.

'So where are you thinking of going then Martone?'

Tommy has returned with a further pint of stout for himself, a Guinness for Martin and a warm, unadorned whisky for each of them.

'The world is my oyster Thomas. Problem is . . . I hate fucking oysters.'

Martin chuckles, chortles and then guffaws. His lone bum cheek threatens to dislodge itself. His whole body quakes and quivers. The slack flab of his neck vibrates. He laughs louder. He starts to cough and choke. He quaffs a gigantic mouthful of Guinness, but his painful laughter doesn't subside. His head lolls grotesquely then falls forward onto his chest. He holds his slabby sides in agony. He starts to keel over to the port side. Tommy manages to stop his imminent fall.

The barman looks over in disgust. Martin is on his final warning in this establishment too, which takes some doing.

'I had better go. I'm collecting . . . collecting . . .'

Martin stalls. The broken laughter subsides. He stares at both his swollen hands.

'I used to play the bass guitar.'

'You still can Martino, you still can . . .'

'How? How?'

Tommy looks at him blankly.

Martin knocks the Scotch back in one.

'I have no bass guitar. No amplifier, no speakers. But Tommy, worst of all . . .'

Martin sobs, it is like a beached killer whale gasping for life.

'. . . I have forgotten all that I once did know . . .'

Martin empties the rest of the dark liquid into his mouth. Some of it dribbles down his unshaven chin; some of it spills over his raincoat.

'Fuckit!'

He suddenly stands to attention and salutes some invisible deity. He staggers rearwards. His tolerance to any chemical be it alcohol or other has been completely shot. He threatens to fall backwards but rights himself at the final instant.

The barman, Tommy and the other two occupants of the public bar all look up at him. He is caught in some transient light. They see the tears glisten in his eyes.

'You have been a wonderful audience. God bless you all . . . thank you . . . and good night.'

He exits.

Martin Hannett has left the building.

He still clutches the ten-pound note like a drowning man clutches a passing log. He could buy a ten-quid wrap. It would be so much better than all the pharmaceutical junk with the antiseptic aftertaste and clinical semi-hallucinations. You can never really nod out properly on that BP stuff, it always interrupts your reverie like a hospital orderly telling you to wake up and go to the day room.

Fortuitously he literally bumps into Dave the Dealer as he rounds the corner. This guy is something of a fan.

'Martin. What the hell has happened to you?'

Martin takes this as a general enquiry.

'I have the ten pounds for the ten-pound wrap.' He betrays his desperation in his voice and face. He owes Dave the D far more than ten pounds.

'This is the last one that I'm ever going to give you Martin. Buy yourself something to eat with that, some fruit and veg; get yourself to rehab, man. You're still young. Go to America and work with those grunge guys. They all love you and the stuff you did with JD and Section 25 and all the young dudes. What are you doing scratting round street corners and terminal saloons in this godforsaken patch?'

It is the longest, most eloquent speech that he has ever spoken. Someone must have written it for him.

'Have you got a ten-quid wrap though, in the mean time?'

Martin gets back to where he resides. It is not home. The flat in Didsbury felt like home for a while, but nowhere since has come close. He tiptoes to the kitchen like some shuffle monster. He finds a piece of crumpled-up tin foil with black smudges all over it. He smoothes it out. He creeps back to his corner by the side of the settee, obscured from passers-by even though the lavender curtains are permanently closed. There is a sodden jade cushion that he sits on, like a pet's favourite place.

Dave the Dealer has gifted him a generous wrap. Martin sees it as a going-away present. His hands are puffy and shaky so it takes him an inordinate amount of time to dish out two thick lines for himself – the entire contents of the present. The ten-pound note comes in handy again. He balances foil, matches and a shred of decorum. It all threatens to collapse but he gets the match lit, the powder heats and smokes and he inhales first one line then the other like a man who has been starved for too long rediscovering the joys of sustenance.

The acrid smoke fills his bronchitic lungs, his wheezy chest and his broken heart. His head lolls and then rolls forward. He drifts off back down the river Memory accompanied by the fanning of a bevy of beauties. Professor Stephen Hopkins is by his side in a pith helmet as they swallow peeled red grapes.

'I'm going to lose some weight, you know, Professor,' he informs the Prof, 'I'm only going to eat an apple and a sarnie a day.' He misses out the bit about loads of amphetamines. It's not that sort of boat trip.

One of the leggy lovelies pours him a phone. He is at his desk at Music Force; he books all his favourite bands for a charity gig.

'I promote a surly, incoherent mass of local talent which encompasses a huge spectrum of skills.'

Professor Hopkins nods sagely. 'And a very good job you make of it too Doctor Hannett.'

The boat begins to gather speed. Other women line the banks throwing garlands of belladonna at him.

He looks to the left bank – John Cooper Clarke and himself are loaded up with substantial recording equipment, they look fresh-faced and glowing, they are making their way to a grotto within which the acoustics are fantastic.

He looks down. Martine is there, smiling sweetly.

'All right?' Martine enquires gently.

There is so much in that 'All right?' – concern, care, empathy, affection.

Her hair is still wet. Her skin is so pale that it looks translucent. Her pale blue eyes linger on and on for ever and ever. She reaches up and places the index finger of her right hand against his moist lips.

'I won't hear the imperfections, Martin. I promise you.'

'I want to be your raincoat for those frequent rainy days; I want to be your dreamboat when you want to sail away. Let me be your teddy bear, take me with you anywhere.'

He whispers to her, quoting Johnny Clarke wholesale. He wants to bend and kiss her cherry-red lips.

He wants to take her deep into his heart, but the boat is in a fast current now heading towards the rapids and then the big waterfall. The hammock slides away, taking her from him. He staggers to the front of the vulnerable little craft. The mast and sail have been blown off. Professor Hopkins has fallen overboard. The lovelies have jumped ship.

All he can see is the approaching waterfall as the boat spins out of control. There is no rudder, no compass. He's lost control again.

He comes back to semi-consciousness with a start. He is covered in sweat. He quickly heats the small amount of heroin that he hasn't smoked.

'Right, down to business,' he mumbles to himself.

There is furniture to be moved. He's not going to let those motherfuckers take his precious bookcase and all that is left of his possessions within.

He stands behind the bookcase. He tries to encircle it with his arms but they're too chubby and short. He begins to walk it across the room towards the doorway that leads upstairs. He still has his raincoat on. Perspiration drips into his eyes. He shoves and heaves. He moves it inch by inch towards the aperture. He raises his face to the heavens. The sweat feels like rain running down his face.

'Clouds collide in the heavens, I surrender to the rain

'The death bells that also rang like madness from above . . .'

He mutters to himself as he pushes with all his might.

'I'm going out with a bang

'And a heart disease called love.'

With a superhuman effort of will, like Chief Broom at the end of *One Flew Over the Cuckoo's Nest* when he tears out the basin, he lifts the bookcase, stumbles forward with it a few paces. It bangs against the door frame. It's too big to fit through, it's too friggin' big.

He loses his grip. The bookcase teeters then the contents start to spill all over him like autumnal leaves scattered by the breeze.

He is covered by invoices, foreign fan mail, record company contracts, original artwork, snapshots of himself playing the crackpot with friends and family and lovers, then his creations begin to rain down on him, they seem to stick into his flabby flesh – the triangular-shaped 'Gimmix' by John Cooper Clarke; the *Innocents* EP on Rabid Records; the beautiful Saville-designed *A Factory Sample* EPs, which stick into each chunky shoulder; John Dowie's egg-shaped disc; *The Return of the Durutti Column*'s sandpaper sleeve grazes his soaked face. His tears mingle with his sweat now. He is trying to stop the heavy piece of furniture from falling on top of him. Then FAC 23, 'Love Will Tear Us

Apart', dislodges itself and slashes down across his chubby cheek. The pain in his chest is unbearable; the pain in his heart is terminal. He looks up, steadies the bookcase for an instant, pushes. It's too big.

'It's too big, too frigging big to fit,' he gasps again.

He lets go. He sees the 12-inch single slowly slide from its pride of place at the top of the prized bookcase.

It is the Sordide Sentimental version of his masterwork 'Atmosphere', pressed as a limited edition of 1,578 with an extravagant three-page sleeve, a lovely photograph of Joy Division taken by Anton Corbijn and a painting of the mourners by Jean-François Jamoul. The 12-inch, sharp-edged vinyl disc, like an obelisk, like the sentinel from *2001*, frees itself from the constraint of its weighty context and flies out and slices into Martin's neck, seeming for an instant to decapitate him, to separate his lolling, mammoth head from his long-suffering body.

The bookcase is wedged in the too, too narrow gap.

James Martin Hannett falls backwards.

The tiny boat without oars or sails topples over the giant waterfall.

The rest is silence.

23

'It's too big. It's too friggin' big to fit.'

The coffin is too big to fit in the grave.

'The frigging coffin is too frigging big to fit in the frigging grave,' some also-ran rants.

It's a line straight out of a John Cooper Clarke witty ditty. It would be a fitting tribute to the man of the moment. Then Wendy 2 jumps on top of the too frigging big coffin in a hysterical attempt to force it into the too frigging small grave.

An equally hysterical Cowboy Dave Rowbotham is still reeling and bug-eyed from the experience of seeing Martin laid out on the mortician's slab like a grotesque beached whale, a carcass ready to rot. Bruce Mitchell, drummer, PA hire guy, entrepreneur and hep cat has taken what is left of him, outlaw guitar slinger, terminal drug addict, Martin clone, to view the Hannett corpse.

It was laid out on the slab, not yet 'touched up'. The face was bloated and slack. The pallor was green and greyish. It bore a striking resemblance to an equally inflated Marlon Brando in the final sequence of *Apocalypse Now*.

Dave took one look at the hideous corpse and literally staggered backwards as if punched in the solar plexus.

'Fuck man, fuck,' Dave spluttered, drooling and dribbling and wiping his hand across his face, trying to clean away the saliva, trying to clear away the horrific image in an unconscious reference to one of Martin's mannerisms. From now until his violent death, less than four months away (the clock is already tick-tocking), he will speak almost entirely in quotations from songs that Martin produced. He will find an old dark green cardigan, as worn by Martin in previous chapters, in a Sue Ryder shop; he will ceaselessly curl his hair around his fingers in an attempt to emulate the iconic hairdo of his Great Man. He will try and learn to play the bass guitar after a lifetime of rhythm guitar. He will sell his beloved Stratocaster and buy a cheap

Fender Precision Bass copy. He will look for girls called Wendy or Suzanne.

Martin's immediate family – his younger brother Mike, his sisters Julie and Elizabeth and his frail and confused father Vincent – look on with disbelief and mounting horror as the grotesque and tragicomic scene unfolds around them. They hold on to each other for support and comfort. They had no idea that all these crazies would be at their brother's, their son's, funeral.

Meanwhile Tosh and Tony, the gruesome twosome, film the whole event for posterity. There are more dead bodies standing around the graveside than there are trying to get in the hole.

'O that this too, too solid earth should melt . . .' one of the failed band of Mancunian thespians gamely chants.

'Alas poor Martin, I knew him well,' ripostes another wrinkly character actor.

It's a who-was-who of the North-West post-punk glitterati. It's a police line-up of every drug dealer in the immediate vicinity. It's the unusual suspects. It's an identity parade for those in danger of permanently losing their identity. The skies open and we surrender to the rain.

Julie Hannett looks around at the gathered ensemble. She looks up at the gathering storm clouds. She looks within at the gathering guilt. The last time that she saw her brother alive was when she put him on a train back to Manchester, with a one-way ticket and the implicit understanding that he wouldn't try and make his way back to their idyll in Wiltshire. He had come to stay, ostensibly to 'clean up' – apparently because Wendy 2 had thrown him out of their house – but within hours he had visited the local public house, discovered the whereabouts of the one neighbourhood drug dealer and was causing mayhem. In the last couple of years the family had stopped providing Martin with cash and postal orders. They had answered his demands for £700 for automobile repairs with a request for the invoice, which had never been forthcoming. It would have broken Mum Veronica's heart.

The authentic mourners, the immediate family, the liggers, the hangers-on, the death watch beetles, gather to gaze, wonder and perhaps reflect on their part (however small) in the killing of Martin Hannett.

Julie links arms with her younger sister Elizabeth. She remembers Martin as a boy carefully taking apart, then reassembling, their grandfather's gramophone player: listening to the collection of priceless recordings on hard black vinyl in their secure brown covers with their distinctive, evocative smell. How he would pore over recordings of the tenor voices of the 1920s and 1930s. Did he know then that he would be drawn to recording mournful tenors himself? Did he imagine that he would be torn apart but not reassembled?

She recalls her older brother as a young teenager, rather chubby and shabby, reading *Hi-Fi News*, taking back every disc that he purchased to the local record shop and demanding a 'better' copy. Julie looks across the grave, which has now been extended so that it can accommodate the extra-large coffin, the earth hacked away by two post-punk henchmen. Wendy is wailing like a banshee. Tosh continues to film the event on Super 8. Tony has taken on the role of director, as ever, suggesting shots and angles and close-ups. Some of the throng cover their faces to avoid the camera.

CP Lee has only seen Martin once in the last ten years and that was ironically merely a week ago. Like many people's last meetings with Martin, it occurred in a pub. Martin seemed upbeat and positive about new projects. CP Lee waits respectfully to read the eulogy in which he will ask people to remember Martin, amongst other things, for his intelligence and sense of humour.

Steve Hopkins can't help feeling guilty that he hasn't seen Martin in the last few years. He wonders, ruefully, if the debacle around the final recording of *Zip Style Method* has in any way contributed to Martin's demise. He keeps thinking of 'Heart Disease Called Love' on that final Cooper Clarke album. How prescient are John's lyrics; how pretty and mournful is the melody; how playfully plodding is Martin's bass line.

The last time they worked together, in 1988, Steve provided some honky-tonk piano for the Happy Mondays' 'Lazyitis' on the *Bummed* album. Martin more or less sleepwalked through those sessions. Supposedly he spent more time in the nearby pub than he did in the studio. Reportedly his belly was so big that he unintentionally knocked all the switches up to 10 when he leaned over the control board, accidentally creating an entire new genre of loved-up, full-on Madchester dance music and endearing him to other bands of a similar ilk.

It is twenty past the hour. A silence befalls the multitude. Each individual has their moment of reflection. Then all eyes turn heavenward.

'Clouds collide in the heavens,
I surrender to the rain.
The death bells that also rang,
Like madness from above,
I'm going out with a bang,
And a heart disease called love.'

You can hear that death bell, that knell, which summons the lapsed soul of the late, great James Martin Hannett to heaven or to hell.

Enter the Dragon; exit Martin Hannett.

As for me, I didn't even know that he had died and only found out a few years later. By then I was clean and sober and trying to forget the past. But I don't believe you can . . .

Epilogue

Fourteen years later, I travel down on the Trans-Pennine Express on my way to the new modish Manchester; the train passes through Stalybridge railway station. I can almost see the ghosts standing on the windswept platform waiting . . . waiting . . . waiting . . .

The last time I saw Martin was in late 1982. When I had last gone to visit him he wasn't in Manchester. He was down in London, trying to save what was left of his career. I had stayed with Suzanne at the Didsbury flat and shared a meal with her, but little else.

I had awoken in the middle of the night – withdrawing, sweaty and shaky – and had padded through to their kitchen. The radiators were humming in harmony with each other. There was a harmony in my head. I opened the fridge and that hummed too. The whole deadened world was humming but I could not place the tune. I wished that Martin was there, sensed that I would never see him again. I decided to visit his office. Turning the light on in the corridor, I felt a shiver down my spine as though I was walking across someone's grave. I opened the office door with a rising sense of foreboding. The light from the hallway eerily illuminated the room. The desk was still there, but cluttered with torn brown envelopes, unpaid invoices, final demands and pages of bank statements, indecipherable contracts and mathematical theorems. The shelves were still loaded with Martin's work – white-label copies, special editions, egg-shaped vinyl, orange triangular 'Gimmix', demo cassettes, double EPs, long letters from obsessive Belgian fans. But it would have been hazardous to reach this cornucopia. Because the entire floor was covered in splinters, shards and slivers of jagged glass. The glass reflected and refracted the light. The glass seemed to be slithering and sliding like snakes. What had he smashed? What had he destroyed? In what tormented state? Why didn't he want anyone, including himself, to have access to his priceless collection? I started to cry. The dead world hummed.

I have had time to reflect on Martin's legacy and enduring influence. I can hear it clearly in the new breed of bands such as Interpol, Editors, Snow Patrol, Franz Ferdinand and The Killers, all of whom acknowledge him and his productions (particularly with Joy Division) as an influence and inspiration. It's always been there in the infrastructure of U2's songs; Simple Minds' sense of space and grandeur; Nirvana's nerve-shredding, auto-depressive attack; Sisters of Mercy's Grand Guignol grandiosity. It is there in the undertow of melancholy and the clean separation of the instruments in so many productions, including Coldplay and Keane. Vin Cassidy, from Section 25, reckoned that Martin 'invented the snare smash'. It is the attention to detail as well. One could argue that Martin was at the birth of punk (with *Spiral Scratch*), post-punk (with *Unknown Pleasures*) and Madchester (with *Bummed*). Not bad going for an old hippy Soft Machine fan.

But the world has also of course moved on without him. Factory Records evolved into FAC 4. Tony married Yvette Livesey, an ex-beauty queen, and has two children. He has become a cultural commentator, a pundit, always ready with a good quote or wry observation or ironic insight and is still sometimes controversial. He still maintains an interest in new groups and retains his fiercely partisan passion for the North-West and has been involved in various regeneration schemes. At the time of writing he is bravely battling cancer, having had one kidney removed. Alan Erasmus and Tony would appear to have drifted apart after the demise of the Haçienda. Alan is often spotted in supermarkets and mentioned in Internet dispatches. He remains the quiet one. Rob Gretton continued to manage and protect the New Order lads right up until his sudden and untimely death. CP Lee is a Professor of Music, a Dylanologist, a great writer and has a huge interest in the history of Manchester cinema. He performs in a ukulele band. Steve Hopkins is also a Professor, of Science. He creates water fountains and, sadly, rarely plays the piano that sits forlornly in his front room. Vini Reilly and manager Bruce Mitchell still perform, irregularly, as The Durutti Column. Bruce still hires out PA equipment. John Cooper Clarke gave up being a performance poet for a while and became a librarian, or so I'm told. These days he is back on the 'circuit', in an erratic fashion. Even his record company don't have his address. He does a very good John Cooper Clarke tribute act.

I'm going down to Manchester to meet up with the remaining members of A Certain Ratio, having made contact with the very gracious and loquacious Martin Moscrop. He is now Head of Music at City College, Salford, just as I am in further education up in Geordie-land. ACR continue to play sporadically and to record together.

In a 2002 interview Jez Kerr from ACR said that 'We thought Martin was a genius, in his own way', to which drummer Donald Johnson added, 'But he didn't fully understand what we were trying to put together. In the same way we didn't understand what he was trying to do.' Wasn't this always the way with Martin and musicians?

I head across Manchester city centre. I thread through an ever busy Arndale Centre. My ghosts rub shoulders with the shoppers. This is where I first saw Martine. She looked like a young Blondie Debbie Harry, her hair peroxide blond, her black jeans skintight. When I fled Manchester in 1981, days after Adam's first birthday – there was no party – Martine stayed and moved back in with her father and then continued to move for the next twenty years.

Martine and I tried to get back together a few times, but our combined drug addictions, our twisted, drug-addled emotions and our mutual deep insecurity made it nigh impossible. It was never acrimonious or unpleasant though and we would sometimes chat on the phone, and I tried to persuade her that it might be an idea to get help and to stop drinking and using, like I had, but she never did. We would meet fleetingly and pass the growing Adam between us, usually at Stalybridge Station.

The last time I saw her she was looking sadly bloated and confused with all the drink, but she still tried to be friendly and helpful and interested and she still had the faintest glimmer of that beautiful look in her beautiful eyes . . .

In 2004, after years of drug addiction, desperation, heartache and galloping alcoholism, Martine Helene eventually succumbed and died on 23 January. She was only 43. It was the same age that Martin had died at. The cause of death was finally given as heart failure, with complications. I went down for her funeral in north Manchester. There was only her immediate family and myself present. It was a grim and godless affair. Her coffin was borne by a horse-drawn hearse and red roses prettily spelt out her pretty name: MARTINE . . . if only I'd held on to your heart.

But I digress . . . as always.

I wend my way to the postmodern palace that is Urbis, an exhibition centre. It strikes me as being something of a shrine to all things Manchester. There is a glass cabinet full of Factoid ephemera – T-shirts, related books, posters and badges. Has Factory Records become just another franchise?

I eat a fabulous post-structuralist hotpot whilst I wait for Martin Moscrop. I'm unsure as to whether we ever met in past lives. I recall bumping into A Certain Ratio, on the bridge that spanned some Manc motorway and led to the hellhole known as Hulme. They did seem very certain in those days, of what I'm not certain myself.

I have warned him that I am wearing a black velvet pinstripe suit and an *Unknown Pleasures* T-shirt, so he spots me easily. He looks far more relaxed, fashionably deconstructed, dressed down and streetwise than me. But that's just hunky and dory. We become more like ourselves as we grow older, *if* we grow older.

As we walk, we talk. Names are mentioned. We establish a shared Factory Records history – however brief. We go back to his terraced house. We are joined by Jez and Donald from ACR. They are extremely helpful. They tell me all that they can recall of their memories of working with Martin Hannett, the record producer. They make it clear that they didn't know Martin Hannett the Man or Martin Hannett the Heroin Fiend. Martin Moscrop has previously told me that he lived close by to Martin Hannett the Terminal Drunk, in his final years, but he tactfully and graciously doesn't refer to that period.

They are candid about the clash of their younger egos with Martin the Autocrat. They speak fondly of their sojourn in New York. They tell me a lovely story about Tony Wilson buying five flat mattresses and bed covers for them to sleep on in the loft that he had hired for their visit. Tony had apparently slept in a separate space by himself. It sounds like a school outing: the geography teacher and his favourite pupils on a field trip. Martin, the grown-up, had stayed in a hotel. They speak warmly of the fantastic job that he had done on the live mix at the club. They are disarmingly frank about how young and naive they were and how Martin seemed somewhat disdainful of that youth and naivety. There is real warmth, affection and sometimes admiration in their recollections. They are realistic too and mention Martin's foibles and idiosyncrasies and how difficult that could be to work with, particularly as they had such strong opinions themselves about how they wanted to sound. On balance it seems to me as though it was a fruitful, creative, mutually beneficial relationship, however fleeting.

Of course the 'Mad Martin' tales are legion and legendary and in most cases semi-fictional. But to paraphrase Tony Wilson, if given the choice between the truth and a good story – always go with the good story. And of course, as his pal CP Lee said, he left 'a bucketful of great recordings'. But let's also remember him for his wit, his intelligence and his wonderful cheeky smile.

So why did Martin die? *What* killed Martin Hannett? There are various opinions and theories. No one believes that it was intentional. It was not suicide. There *is* a history of heart failure in his family. But everyone agrees that the combination of years of drink, drug and food abuse and his extreme obesity in the last years of his life must have contributed greatly to his comparatively young death. Perhaps one of the greatest contributing factors to Martin's death, apart from the obvious ones of drink, drugs and far too much cholesterol, was that he had lost his way. He had separated himself from what he really loved and what motivated him – going into a recording studio with a bunch of keen musicians and creating something incredible and eternal. He lost the creative part of himself and without that creative energy, replaced by the deadening effects of alcohol and fat and methadone, there was little to keep him alive. Eventually, perhaps, it was simple: not being in the studio killed him . . .

In present-day Manchester, the members of ACR and I take our leave of each other. They have football matches to watch, ice hockey to spectate; new, fresh, vital records to make. I have a Trans-Pennine locomotive express to catch and travel back up, passing through Stalybridge railway station, to Newcastle.

I leave behind memories, and ghosts.

Related books

Antonia, Nina, *The One and Only: Peter Perrett – Homme Fatale* (SAF, 1996)

Bockris, Victor, *Transformer: The Lou Reed Story* (Simon & Schuster, 1995)

Boyd, Joe, *White Bicycles* (Serpent's Tail, 2006)

Buckley, Peter (ed.), *The Rough Guide to Alternative Rock* (Penguin, 2003)

Bussy, Pascal, *Kraftwerk* (SAF, 1993)

Cavanagh, John, *The Piper at the Gates of Dawn* (Continuum, 2003)

Cawthorne, Nigel, *The Making of The Stone Roses* (Unanimous, 2005)

Cohen, Nik, *Awopbopaloobopalopbam-boom* (Pimlico, 1969)

Cross, Charles, *Heavier than Heaven: Kurt Cobain* (Hodder and Stoughton, 2001)

Curtis, Deborah, *Touching from a Distance* (Faber and Faber, 1995)

Flowers, Claude, *New Order and Joy Division* (Omnibus, 1995)

Harvard, Joe, *The Velvet Underground and Nico* (Continuum, 2004)

Haslam, Dave, *Manchester, England* (Fourth Estate, 1999)

——, *Not Abba* (Fourth Estate, 2005)

Hayman, Ronald, *The Death and Life of Sylvia Plath* (Sutton, 2003)

Heylin, Clinton, *Form and Substance* (Sound, 1988)

Hoskins, Barney, *Waiting for the Sun* (Penguin, 1996)

Johnson, Mark, *An Ideal for Living* (Proteus, 1984)

King, Emily (ed.), *Designed by Peter Saville* (Frieze, 2003)

Lee, CP, *Shake, Rattle and Rain* (Hardinge Sinpole, 2002)

Marcus, Greil, *Like a Rolling Stone* (Faber and Faber, 2005)

McDonald, Ian, *Revolution in the Head* (Pimlico, 1998)

Middles, Mick, *From Joy Division to New Order* (Virgin, 2002)

——, *Shaun Ryder: Happy Mondays, Black Grape and Other Traumas*

(Independent Music Press, 1997)
—— and Lindsay Reade, *Torn Apart* (Omnibus, 2006)
Miles, Barry, *In the Sixties* (Pimlico, 2003)
Morley, Paul, *Nothing* (Faber and Faber, 2000)
——, *Words and Music* (Fourth Estate, 2005)
Murray, Charles Shaar, *Crosstown Traffic* (Faber and Faber, 1989)
——, *Shots from the Hip* (Penguin, 1991)
Neal, Charles, *Tape Delay* (SAF, 1987)
Niven, John, *Music from Big Pink* (Continuum, 2005)
Ott, Chris, *Unknown Pleasures* (Continuum, 2004)
Palacios, Julian, *Lost in the Woods: Syd Barrett and the Pink Floyd* (Boxtree, 1998)
Paytress, Mark, *Vicious: The Art of Dying Young* (Sanctuary, 2004)
Rawlings, Terry, *Brian Jones: Who Killed Christopher Robin?* (Helter Skelter, 1994)
Reynolds, Simon, *Rip It Up and Start Again* (Faber and Faber, 2005)
Savage, Jon, *England's Dreaming* (Faber and Faber, 1991)
——, *Time Travel* (Vintage, 1997)
Tamm, Eric, *Brian Eno: His Music and the Vertical Color of Sound* (Da Capo Press, 1995)
Thompson, Dave, *Beautiful Chaos: The Psychedelic Furs* (Helter Skelter, 2004)
——, *True Faith* (Helter Skelter, 2005)
——, *Wall of Pain: The Biography of Phil Spector* (Sanctuary, 2003)
West, Mike, *Joy Division* (Babylon Books, 1984)
Wilcken, Hugo, *Low* (Continuum, 2005)
Wilson, Tony, *24 Hour Party People* (C4, 2002)

Albums produced by Martin Hannett

John Cooper Clarke, *Disguise in Love* (CBS, 1978)
John Cooper Clarke, *Snap, Crackle and Bop* (CBS, 1980)
John Cooper Clarke, *Zip Style Method* (CBS, 1982)
Joy Division, *Unknown Pleasures* (Factory Records, 1979)
Joy Division, *Closer* (Factory Records, 1980)
Joy Division, *Still* (Factory Records, 1981)
New Order, *Movement* (Factory Records, 1981)
Magazine, *The Correct Use of Soap* (Virgin, 1980)
The Durutti Column, *The Return of the Durutti Column* (Factory Records, 1980)
Happy Mondays, *Bummed* (Factory Records, 1988)
A Certain Ratio, *To Each . . .* (Factory Records, 1981)
A Certain Ratio, *Early* (Soul Jazz Records, 2002)
Section 25, *Always Now* (Factory Records, 1981)
The Names, *Swimming* (Crepuscule, 1982)
Basement 5, *1965–1980* (Antilles, 1980)
Pauline Murray and The Invisible Girls, *Pauline Murray and The Invisible Girls* (Illusive, 1980)
Jilted John, *True Love Stories* (EMI, 1978)
Magazine, *Magic, Murder and the Weather* (Virgin, 1981)

Three compilations of Martin's productions have been issued – the third and most recent is probably the best:

Martin (Factory Records, 1992)
And Here Is the Young Man: Martin Hannett Productions 1978–1991 (Polygram, 1998)
Zero: A Martin Hannett Story 1977–1991 (Big Beat, 2006)

Thanks to . . .

in no particular order,
Simon Reynolds (*Rip It Up and Start Again*)
Peter Saville (Designed by . . .)
Jon Savage (*England's Dreaming*)
Mick Middles (*Torn Apart*)
James Nice (LTM)
Tony Wilson (Factory Records)
Nick Halliwell (musician and writer)
Mick Griffiths and all at Renascent Records
Kitty Fitzgerald (writer)
Kevin Conroy Scott (literary agent/writer)
Adam Sharp (my son and rock writer)
Natasha Martin (my editor)
Celia Hayley (my other editor)
Emily Sharp (my daughter)
Grace Sharp (my daughter)
Donna Tonkinson (mother of my daughters)
Tony McMahon (Australian journalist/writer)
Bruce Mitchell (drummer supreme)
Michael Mitchell (no relation)
Stephen Hopkins (Invisible Girl)
Martin MacAloon (Prefab Sprout)
Vini Reilly (The Durutti Column)
Tosh Ryan (Rabid Records)
CP Lee (*Shake, Rattle and Rain*)
Lee Brackstone (Faber)
Clive Frayne (writer/director)
Valerie Hopper (ex-girlfriend)

Debbie Curtis (*Touching from a Distance*)
Alan Wise (promoter/manager)
Phil Jones (manager, The Durutti Column)
Martin Moscrop (ACR)
Jez (ACR)
Donald Johnson (ACR)
Big T (Happy Mondays fan)
Michael Eastwood (many pies)
Robert Blamire (Penetration/Invisible Girls)
Pauline Murray (Penetration/vocalist supreme)
John Cooper Clarke (Bard of Salford)
Nick Holmes (radio)
Ged Murray (photographer)
Julie Hannett (Martin's sister)
Ben aka Neil aka Stavross (sic) (Haçienda door staff)
Ozit aka Chris Hewitt (Ozit Records)
Pete Farrow (authentic singer-songwriter)
Alan Pryor (wore a cloak)
Michael Farnell (New Fast Automatic Daffodils tour manager)
Tony Ogden (The High)
Steve Fitzpatrick (a good contact)
Kevin Hewitt (singer-songwriter)
Andy McCluskey (OMD)
John (Kitchens of Distinction)
Howard Devoto (Magazine)
Raine Marcus (returned angel)
Daniel Meadows (photographer)
Pat Gilbert (*Passion is a Fashion*)

Index